The Infinite One

A Closer Look at the Nature of Our Universe, and What It Tells Us About Healthy Ways of Being

A. Grateful Human

ISBN-13: 9798668152858

Library of Congress Control Number: 2020915119

Cover design by: A. Grateful Human

Printed in the United States of America, Bolingbrook IL

10 9 8 7 6 5 4 3

Dedicated to the seekers, the doubters, the lovers, and the dreamers

Table of Contents:

Introduction

Hello and greetings, fellow human! This book is intended to be a guided reflective meditation that helps you explore questions around the past, present, and future conditions of your life and the nature of the universe that surrounds you. It adds some context around things believed to be true through the wisdom of thousands of scientists, philosophers, spiritual leaders and others over thousands of years. The tone of this book is conversational, contemplative, and probing. Any numbers or information contained within it are not intended to be authoritative or comprehensive. Rather, they are used to provide a base to introduce the reader to some naturally complex topics and provide a point from which to further discuss or consider. For instance, there is still ongoing, healthy debate on many aspects of early life forms and their origins. It is also still unclear exactly how big or old the universe really is. For the purposes of this book, the idea that all living species do share a common ancestral life form -- or that the universe is very, very big and old -- are the main areas of focus. While reading, please realize that there are several finer points within the big ideas that continue to be explored, debated, and updated with time.

Additionally, to honor the conversational tone and invoke curiosity, the names of all scientists and references to sources of stated information have been intentionally omitted. This book is above all about "we," so breaking down contributions by recognizing name, institution, gender, age, race, or any other identifying factor is not relevant in this context. The most important realization is that together, as a species, we have discovered some of nature's most important telling features. It is not intended to slight or disrespect in any way the decades of work many scientists and others have dedicated to careful study, experimentation, and publication. For those interested, a quick search around topics discussed in the book will point you to some of the sources considered to be authoritative. I am extremely grateful for all members of our species who have contributed to our current body of knowledge and wisdom, expressed in so many varied and beautiful ways, who keep our collective experience unfolding in the way it does.

Get involved! Any suggested changes and feedback for future editions of the book are welcome. Please send an email to: theinfiniteonebook@gmail.com

Prologue

It was a cold, windy and overcast February day when I died. The streets and houses around me felt deserted and desolate -- so dead, just like me. It all felt so fitting. My wife and two kids were out of the house as I lay curled up in the fetal position on our bed, wrapped tight in a blanket to shield myself from the outside world. I had spared them the sight of my death as my eyes were closed, putrid-smelling sweat excreting from my skin as I quietly breathed shallow breaths, feeling my body shake as I clenched my fists and jaw. But my lungs maintained their breathing, and my heart continued its beating as a part deep inside of me -- somewhere formless and timeless -- grew agitated, restless, and distant. Then, it breathed its last gasp. That part of me was dying, escaping like a dark vapor of smoke, yet still here I was. I was still alive. As I slowly made my way from out of the covers, I opened my eyes and the diffuse sunlight had a sort of pink glow of which I had not seen before. The moments that followed began to take on a new quality, and it would take some time for me to unpack what had just happened.

Leading up to that day, I had been listening to a scripted, internal illusion most all my life that I believed so adamantly in my heart to be the truth, but alas, it was not. As I laid in that bed, these illusions were strong and running through my mind while bumping up against what was truly real. Either the illusions or I had to die. You see, a history of unhealthy thought and heart patterns led me to the conclusion that because I had failed in creating a successful business that had money, time, and opportunity cost attached to it, my life was meaningless, insignificant, and a big disappointment. Anything I had done in the past was of no consequence. I thought everyone, including my loving family, would be much better off without this mistake of a human being taking up extra room on this planet. I felt ashamed, apathetic, weak, powerless, and spiteful. But what was the illusion that had led up to my feelings that day?

The illusion was that I was special, more special, than others around me. The illusion was that good things happening to me were fair and deserved, and unfair things were either my or somebody else's fault. The illusion was that I was more gifted, smarter, more talented, and more capable of achieving whatever I set my mind to as compared to others around me. The illusion was that I was only deserving of love when I did something others saw as good. The illusion was that my worth was tied to the money I made. The illusion was that my goodness was conditional, subjectively conditional, on how things unfolded according to the plans I had intention of carrying out. The illusion was that my past failures must be carried with me into my "now" moment, and my future moments were something I should be able to control if only I exerted the right effort in the right places. The illusion was that I could operate on my own merits and abilities as a virtual self-sufficient island, psychologically pushing most everyone away as I became jealous of anyone who knew something I did not or did something I deemed as better.

Many of these illusions I knew to be such on a mental, intellectual level, or from reading or hearing it from others. However, the energy of my heart and internal being did not know, leaving my mind and body in confused disarray. Though these illusions helped kill my ego, since that death I have never felt more alive, awake, and connected to myself and all of life. Each day I strive to put myself in position to awaken just a little bit more to the true beauty and sacredness of what is around me. I feel myself distancing from my birth name and ego and aligning more with simply being A. Grateful Human. Getting rid of unhealthy illusions in both heart and mind is a much-needed process I feel every human is worthy and deserving of, resulting in a magnificent freedom that cannot be fully described -- only experienced.

This book highlights some ways you can change and expand areas of focus so you can more readily recognize harmful illusions you may hold about your life, origin, connection to others, and purpose. A few of the most important and undeniable physical truths we have discovered as a human race that underpin our reality are summarized. I believe the implications of these realities point us to a pathway of lasting peace, health, and readiness with each other. This book will challenge you to view yourself in the context of all spaces and times, as a balanced and mysterious collection of forces, as an individual with perspectives only you can access, as a small but indispensable link in the billions-of-years long chain of life, and as an important cell within the network of life as you move gracefully toward your bodily death. It implores you to rethink your ideas of chaos and order, good and bad, life and death, and what is really meant by the concept of free will. It has been written for both the theist and atheist, for the non-scientist and science-minded, and for most anyone who is ready to enhance their cosmic and spiritual perspective.

In the end, this book is intended to help preserve and advance over time one possible framework for making sense of life and what we are to do with our precious brief time here. This framework is just one approach out of an infinite many that can point you to a better understanding of a love and power far beyond us. Once we are together able to see ourselves, other life, and other things around us as truly sacred, as well as both infinite and one, I believe we are in a position to make progress much more efficiently around many issues including racial and gender inequality, war, governmental structures, economic disparity, environmental degradation, and the idea of personal ownership. To get there, however, takes a willingness to look unabashedly at "what is" as opposed to focusing on stubborn illusions that will slowly kill the collective energy of our spirits and ability to connect with what is around and within us in the present moment. It is about being and staying in a curious and wondrous state of readiness, right now. Are you ready for your next moment? Then let us begin.

x

Chapter 1: Space and Time

Where Are You?

Do you know where you are right now? Where would you say you are physically located? You might answer the room or building you are inside, the name of the city in which you are, or that you are nearby to some geographic reference point. Your vision system tends to keep focus on spaces not too far away from you, so that is what you usually hold closest to your attention. But really, where are you? And how do you know where you are? On the surface, perhaps this question seems a bit trivial -- you might be tempted to say that you know exactly where you are and how to get from place to place, or perhaps you feel like you are comfortable with whatever answer you are giving because you or your family have a long history with a certain place. On a day-to-day basis, you probably do not spend too much time worrying about where you are, unless it is a new location and you are trying to find your way through somewhere unfamiliar. If you are of a more technical nature, you might want to answer the question by mentioning longitudinal and latitudinal coordinates, as well as an elevation above sea level with tight precision. Yet, however you answer the question, you are probably using Earth as its own reference, and possibly referencing the sun, moon, or North Star. Measures of distances and directions you usually think about are all relative to something else on the surface of the Earth. After all, this is what you are largely familiar with, as some part of the Earth's surface has consistently been in view for you since the time of your birth, so it would make sense to think in this way.

What if the question was tweaked a bit to ask collectively "Where are we?" We might say that we are on Earth. But that still does not answer the question entirely. We dig one layer deeper and ask where Earth is. Since the dawn of humanity, we have gazed in awe at the sky and wondered what is out there. It is as if the sky were intentionally there just to entice us to probe its nature and help us to realize our smallness. Looking up at a clear night sky can remind us how much is beyond our latitudes and longitudes, our distances north or east of an ocean. Generations have been mesmerized by the moon, the sun, the planets, and beyond. Unfortunately, even as more sophisticated telescopes that look deeper and clearer into the universe are developed, the question of where we are cannot be answered in a definitive way. The best we can ever do is give a relative distance and direction from something else. We can say that the North Star is about 323 light-years in a straight-line distance away from the Earth -- that is, that it would take a beam of light, which travels at the fastest speed allowable in our universe, 323 years to travel between the North Star and Earth. We can also state we are about 25,000 light-years in a straight-line distance away from the center of the Milky Way Galaxy, an enigmatic collection of billions of stars and planets that spans about 100,000 light-years across. If we zoom out even more, we can measure distances between galaxies and say that we are about 2.5 million light-years away from the Andromeda Galaxy, the one nearest to our home Milky Way Galaxy. We zoom out one more time and we find that everything we can possibly observe in the universe contains as much as two trillion of these galaxies, each containing billions of stars, planets, gas clouds, and more. In other words, there is no shortage of things in different places or at different distances for us that we have found in space.

Now let us ask one last time -- we are on the Earth, which is in our solar system, which is in the Milky Way Galaxy, which is situated among numerous other galaxies, so then where are all these galaxies exactly? Over a hundred years ago, we sought out to establish a "still" framework for space itself by measuring relative movements to it. To understand what was trying to be accomplished, we can use a ship on an ocean as a metaphor. We might realize that to figure out how quickly we might reach a distant island we are headed toward, we need to know not just the speed of the ship relative to the water, but also the speed of the water relative to the island. In this case, we would think of the ground connected to the island as being our "still" reference point to which we would measure the ship's true speed of island approach. In a similar way, we wanted to know a "still" reference to measure the Earth's movement to space itself. If Earth was the ship moving through space which is acting as the water, how quickly were the Earth and space moving relative to one another? To what can we anchor space? So, to help answer this question, the time for beams of light to travel set distances in different directions was measured, and the resulting times were all identical. This result made no intuitive sense and is similar to saying that for the ship and island example, no matter what direction the water is travelling and how fast it carries the ship with it, the ship's speed as it heads to the island is always the same. If the water current is going in the direction of the ship, or against it, the ship reaches the island at the same time, every time. Anyone who has run with or against the wind immediately knows the feeling of it helping you speed up or slow down, but in this case it is as if it would have no effect at all.

This result was very perplexing, because it all but guaranteed that we would never be able to have a longitude or latitude type of coordinate for space itself. This result led us to the conclusion that the nature of space itself is relative only and not absolute. It is like a universe that has only numerous ships on a placid ocean that never ends, with no land or sea features to reference. The best that can be done is to reference the ships with each other to describe their locations. So as far as we can tell, there is no end to space itself. There is a limit to how far away we can observe things from Earth, which stands to be about 13.8 billion light-years, but we do not know and cannot know what is beyond that because of the age of the universe and the speed at which light can travel. There is no light particle, or any form of electromagnetic radiation (such as microwaves, x-rays, etc.), that has reached us from such distances to help bring definition to the space beyond that distance, but the space might still exist.

Consider the delay that is present between a bolt of lightning and the thunder that follows. We see the flash of lightning, but then it can be some time before we hear the thunder, especially if the storm is further away. It could be said that we are listening into the past then, as the sound was created the moment of the lightning strike, but it did not reach our ears until later. However, to someone very close to the lightning strike, the sound is much more closely aligned with the current moment. This same type of phenomenon happens with light waves and is how we define space from the vantage point of Earth. One of the big reasons we believe the universe began 13.8 billion years ago is because of the distance of the furthest light we can detect. Similar to the thunder example, though, if we were located on the furthest object we can detect, the sky would look very different, and presumably we would be able to detect light from further distances in space than we are able to on Earth. Until time passes, we are "deaf" to the thunder and we cannot possibly know about it. In the same way, we are "blind" to light that is beyond a certain distance from us. This leaves us in a condition where we are unable to say precisely where the beginning or end of space is, and nature has been structured in such a way that causes us to theorize and guess about it.

Though space itself may be endless, there is something very special and sacred about the space that commonly answers the question "Where are we?" in relation to Earth. Treating the universe as a sphere 13.8 billion light-years in radius, our entire Earth is one part in 10^{57} (or a 1 followed by 57 zeros, so one part out of 1,000,000,000,000,000,000,000,000,000,000, 000,000,000,000,000,000,000,000,000) of the volume of that universe. It is theorized the universe is even larger than 13.8 billion light-years in radius, in which case the Earth would be but one part in an even larger number! One part in 10^{57} is unlike anything we are familiar with in everyday life. To give an idea of just how small that is, one person on Earth represents about one part in 10^{10}, as does one second of time in the life of someone who lives to be 100 years. One cell in your body represents about one part in 10^{13}, or 1,000 times smaller than one in 10^{10}. One grain of sand compared to all sand grains on Earth gets us to about one part in 10^{18}. One molecule of water represents about one part in 10^{47} when talking about all the water in Earth's oceans. Only when we estimate the volume of a single quark, which is the smallest known particle that makes up matter, almost unimaginably small in size, in relation to the volume of your entire body do we start to approach one part in 10^{57}. Remember, though, we are talking about the entire Earth in relation to the universe. When we start to talk about the space that *you* take up, relative to the universe, we start to see numbers less than one part in 10^{75}. Comparisons get even trickier at this point!

When numbers get as big as the ones we are considering, they start to lose meaning when trying to attach them to our human experience. Nonetheless, the greater point is this -- that the space you take up and observe around you is so incredibly precious, so incredibly rare, so incredibly personal, and so incredibly distinct when considering the whole of what we know is out there. We are left to continually guess at just how rare the space is that we occupy and will never have any clue as to where that space really is in a cosmological sense. We cannot know in an absolute way how we fit into the bigger, more complex and complete picture in space. You may not feel that the place you live is particularly special, or the space your body inhabits is in any way remarkable, but these spaces are so much so. Recognizing this, it is fitting to practice honoring and marveling at the presence of the space we experience around us, at all times and in all situations. The shapes that help give it definition, the movements within it, the way colors and trees and clouds appear in space -- it is all overwhelmingly incredible that we get the chance to experience it. We can carry this realization with us to help foster our gratitude and joy for all that we see and observe in the space of the world around us. On one hand, the spaces we experience are small and insignificant compared to the entirety of all space, yet on the other hand, they are unique and custom made to allow for our human experiences. Space -- how humbling, special, magnificent, and glorious! Take a moment to look around you and drink it in. Space, as a compassionate and selfless giver, holds us and all we know in its essence.

What Time Is It?

Do you know about what time it is for you right now? Morning? Evening? What day of the week it is? What month you are in? What year it is? You are probably able to answer these questions right now pretty quickly. In most parts of the world, our minds have been trained very well to think of these answers in terms of a calendar that counts about 365.25 rotations of the Earth on its own axis (each one we call a "day") as it makes one complete revolution around the sun (what we call a calendar "year"). This is the most common way, though some calendars focus on moon cycles instead. So many things depend on the rhythm of the week, which is just a collection of seven days, and the rhythm of the month, another collection of a set number of days. Many take comfort in segmenting time in this way, as it provides humanity a shared structure and pattern around these rhythms. It helps many to set goals and milestones like, "This week I'm going to make sure I get extra sleep" or "This month I'm going to limit my sugar intake." From businesses to schools to events, so much depends on clinging to the shared idea of the week, the month, or the year. If someone tells us they went somewhere last Tuesday, there is a shared idea of what that means. However, when we take it down to its core, it is a somewhat arbitrary counting system that uses relative positions and movements of the sun. Dividing things up into seven-day weeks has its origin in the number of celestial bodies seen in the sky, dividing things up into twelve months was due to moon cycles, and the number of the year, for most, references the birth of Jesus. However, this was not always the case. Although most historical timekeeping methods included days, lunar cycles, and solar years, just a few thousand years ago people would have stared at you blankly if you told them about something that happened during "June 22nd, which was a Tuesday." It may have meaning to us now, but it does not really get at what time *really* is.

In a similar way, many of us have definition around what an hour, a minute, or a second feel like, but these delineations were not always defined as such until hundreds of years ago. Eventually, the day was divided up into 24 equal parts of time passage -- 12 of them before the day's middle (or ante meridian - a.m.) and twelve of them after (or post meridian - p.m.). This number was used because it corresponded to the same number of months in a year and could be further evenly divided up into halves, thirds, fourths, sixths, and eighths. It was a convenient number. The minute and the second were further divided into parts of 60 because of the ease of keeping track of this number using your hands to count. If you use your thumb on one hand to touch each segment of your four fingers, you get 12, and if you keep track of these sets of 12 with your other hand's fingers, you can keep track of up to 12 times 5, or 60. This is all to say that the very definitions of time we hold so close to us and ours ways of life are based mostly on things in the sky, the easy divisibility of certain numbers, and the shape of our own hands.

This system reduces to a convenient, agreed upon counting system for tracking where we are in space relative to the sun and relative to a defined cyclic start and end point -- where a new calendar year begins -- as we revolve around it. Once we say "It's 3:35 a.m. on Saturday, July 28," this is not so much an entirely new thing called "time", per se, as it is rather a declaration of where exactly the Earth is in space at that moment, and a way to separate cause from effect. Putting the two together we can create a concept of "spacetime" to describe our universe, where there are three dimensions of space and one dimension of time. We are able to count space by perceiving distances and count time by perceiving seconds. Both feel very real to us, lend meaning to our lives, and tend to not warrant too much disagreement. However, just like space, even though we can perceive and measure time we cannot say in an absolute way what it really is – other than something required for events or movements to unfold.

The same fundamental limitation with trying to measure the total scope of space in an absolute way also arises when we try to measure the total scope of time in an absolute way. Just like we have the limitation of sensing the whole rest of the universe from the vantage point of Earth and cannot establish when we are located in space in an absolute way, we can only guess at the whole of time from the vantage point of now. We are constantly bound to what we call the present, forever. Life will only ever be real to us right now. Every single moment that already happened, or that is about to happen, is not real in the same way the present is. Like space, when we ask the question "What time is it?" and seek to get an absolute answer, we can only reference other times around it, but we cannot establish a beginning or an end. You might be thinking -- but wait, we know that the universe began about 13.8 billion years ago, so that is a beginning! There is a big problem with this, though. From what is theorized, the earliest moments of the universe were extremely unstable in a physical sense, and this thing called "time" really had little meaning at that point as the universe expanded at an unfathomable rate. There is little reason to believe that time passage was as uniform as we perceive it today. For example, imagine you used a stopwatch to measure the amount of time that unfolded between a cyclic event, say the sun rising and setting today, and it read 12 hours. So, at the end of this, you conclude that a day is represented by 12 stopwatch hours of sun. Tomorrow, though, you measure that same cycle and instead your stopwatch reads 30 seconds or 500 hours though everything is functioning properly. Your representation of a day being equal to 12 hours is now inconsistent and loses meaning. Under more extreme conditions, nature allows for this type of ambiguity, so we really cannot say "when" the universe began and capture those earliest moments completely. What we refer to as the first "year" that the universe was in existence could have been counted on a stopwatch (if in theory it was able to even exist in those conditions) as 20 seconds or 500 trillion years.

Take a moment to recognize that in an absolute, cosmic sense, we can never know where or when we are. We are simply existing in a very mysterious and infinite mesh of spacetime. The best answer we can ever hope to give to "where are you?" is to say "here," and to the question "what time is it?" is to say "now." It is powerful to continually remind yourself of that. It is all you will ever have and all you will ever be given. It is always where we are locked in. Just as with the incredible smallness of space we perceive in relation to what we believe is the whole, the smallness and specialness of the now moment is conceivably even greater. Each precious second, if we assume time to have been always consistent, represents about one part in 10^{18} of all the time known -- like one grain of sand amongst all the grains on the Earth. How rare and remarkable are each one of these passing seconds! "Right now" is our most precious gift and why we sometimes refer to it as "the present."

If we are not appreciating every second as it passes, adding up to an unimaginably vast stack of "presents," it becomes tough to truly recognize just how incredibly rich we already are, and how much we continue to receive. The "here *and* the now," taken together as the ultimate spacetime rarity, draws no conceptual comparison to anything we can ever count or imagine. Now that is a gift to enjoy!

It's All Relative

Gravity is an amazing thing -- it is a pull that keeps us and so many other things attracted to each other and keeps us in those special spaces we enjoy on Earth. Without gravity, our space would not have been able to pull together enough space dust to make any planets, including the Earth. Yet this pull of gravity tells us even more about the nature and specialness of spacetime. To get a visual about how gravity works, imagine for a moment a store giving away free chunks of extremely valuable gold. Even better, this supply is not limited. They proclaim this loudly from the store, and everyone nearby immediately drops what they are doing to head straight for the store. As more people head to the store, those around them are told what is happening, and they also head to the store. People who previously had no interest in doing this see the excitement and cannot be the ones missing out, so they join the rush. We know that if this were a real-life scenario, people would grab their gold and head back, and if crowds were too large around the store, many would turn around for practical reasons. Imagine for a moment, though, that there was nothing to drive people away, or even more, once they started heading for the store, they simply could not turn around and had to get as close to the store as possible and stay there forever. Over time, as the crowd around the store grows, eventually every person on Earth heads to the store, no matter how far away they are. Two main ideas that are parallel to how gravity works apply here; first, a solely attractive force exists, and second, the greater the amount of matter involved, the greater the strength of the force created.

This pull of gravity, in theory, acted over several billion years' worth of time to keep pulling together more and more dust and chunks of matter in space that floated nearby to help form early Earth over 4 billion years ago. It has pulled together just enough matter such that everything can exist just the way it is. It is just enough gravity for our human bodies to operate in the way they do, just enough for all Earth's life forms to exist in their present form, and just enough to allow for the formation of all our rivers, mountains, oceans, and weather system. Just enough for us to be able to build dwellings that do not fall, or for birds and aircraft to take flight in the sky. In our human existence on Earth, gravity is a perfect ally for which we should be very thankful. If it pulled on everything in the universe just a bit weaker, planets and stars would not have formed. If it pulled on everything in the universe just a bit harder, galaxies would be collapsing in on themselves.

Much like a well-meaning person coming into a leadership position, with gravity first everything starts out generally friendly and with good intentions. Once that leader gains too many followers and success though, they might reach a point where they become a controlling dictator if not kept in check by appropriate forces. Consider how quickly life would change if there were more and more things for the Earth to pull in, so that it became double, triple, or even 1,000 times the size of what it is today. In this case, anything on the surface would be pulled in so much harder -- trees, mountains and our bones alike would not be able to stabilize at all. And since the Earth's size is now so much greater, it pulls everything around it even harder, attracting even more with time. At this point, as far as we can tell, life would not be able to exist and the very atoms that hold everything together start to pull closer and closer together, condensing everything. Gravity would become the controlling monopoly of Earth to which everything else would submit. At some point, this fictitious oversized Earth begins to get smaller in size, but its pull is just as powerful. The pull starts to become so strong that anything getting close enough to it, even a beam of light, cannot escape and gets sucked inside. Once this point is reached, we call this entity a black hole, and as far as we know, there are potentially trillions of these that exist in the known universe. The amount of matter they have inside can vary widely, but in all cases, they defy anything we experience here on Earth. The most massive black hole discovered so far has swallowed the equivalent mass of about 10^{38} people, 10^{16} (10 quadrillion) earths, or 10^{10} (ten billion) suns, and this is merely one black hole!

Black holes do more than just swallow up lots and lots of mass; they also to a very significant degree affect the spacetime around them. If you get close enough to a black hole, space and time themselves start to change form. We take for granted the seemingly trivial notion that if given the same measuring tool, two people would quickly agree on distances between two objects or the time between two events. When getting close to black holes, or travelling close to the speed of light, there instead is disparity on these things. Objects subjected to gravitational fields or high speeds of travel experience a compaction of measured space and time. Both conditions produce similar effects. To help understand this idea, think about your perception of distance. In your field of vision, things further away look smaller, and we realize that those things appear to change size as they change their distance from us. Imagine you do an experiment with two friends who are exactly the same height as you; one who is influenced by a stronger and stronger gravitational field as they walk away from you, and one who is not. All three of you are on an open field. When you stand together, you agree that you all have the same height. The two friends then move the same distance away. As they walk side by side, backs to you, the one not influenced by gravity looks like they are half their original height, but the influenced one looks to be just one fourth of their original height. Yet, everyone would maintain from their point of reference that they are still their original height. The stronger the gravity, the greater this perceived disparity between the two friends. In the most extreme case, as your gravitationally influenced friend walks away, they literally disappear from sight as the other one remains in plain view.

You use binoculars, a telescope, or any tool to look in the area of your friend, but they appear to have simply vanished.

Let us reimagine this thought experiment a bit differently to consider what happens with time. You all begin at the same spot, carrying perfectly functioning stopwatches, and begin them at the same instant. Again, the two friends walk away from you and eventually work their way back. You compare the time on the stopwatches once all three of you are together again. The friend not influenced by the strong gravity during this time and you both have a reading of exactly one hour. However, the friend who was influenced shows their stopwatch and it reads only thirty minutes. That friend really experienced less time than you between the events, meaning that their body aged only thirty minutes while yours aged one hour. You could say they were able to take a shorter travel time because during their trip, from your perspective, they moved through compacted space so they were able to move more quickly through it. For them, however, in the space immediately around them they notice nothing unusual. As gravity gets stronger and stronger, this difference is more pronounced, and your one hour becomes ten minutes for them, then one minute, then one second. As your friend looks back at you, you appear to slow down more and more. As they watch you for just one of their minutes, you biologically age 50 years. In the most extreme case, under a massive amount of gravity, in the smallest fraction of a second the entirety of all future times unfolds for them. For them, time itself stops. For you, they are frozen forever, never to return.

When pondering that gravity or your rate of movement affects your perception of space and time, it may feel like science fiction. It may be difficult to connect this to your everyday experience. However, these effects are very real and have been well-documented through observation of very precise clocks on airplanes and even cars measuring slightly longer time intervals than identical clocks on the ground. Our entire global positioning system (GPS), which is comprised of several moving satellites, must be continually recalibrated to account for these effects so that they can give accurate location information. The presence of these differences further entrench the strangeness of our universe and allow us to appreciate that even our perception of spacetime is not a foundation we can rely on to be true in an absolute sense. Gravity and black holes are concepts that can teach us about the relative nature of experiences possible in our universe. Gravity gives birth to black holes -- places we can investigate and where we can literally stare into an infinite spacetime.

We have no clue what it is like to be inside of one and may never know. Interestingly, black holes are essential and even central to our existence, though. To create any stable galaxy, any stable place where stars and planets collect, there must be a black hole in the center about which everything else revolves. In fact, we are revolving around one right now that sits in the center of the Milky Way Galaxy. Black holes are the centerpieces on the cosmic table -- violent, destructive, intense and ruthless to anything that comes near. But at the same time, when you are far enough away, they can be creative, loving, humbling, life-giving, and benign to us. However you want to look at the nature of black holes and the gravity needed to create them, it's all relative.

Think for a moment how physical and emotional perceptions differ, as well as likes and dislikes, between any two people. Two people eat the same meal: while one thinks it is the tastiest thing ever, the other could not care less for it. One person is eager to swim in a river while another is absolutely terrified to do so. One person is inspired by a leader while another despises that same individual. One person gets angry or nervous whenever seeing a dog while another lovingly moves to pet and connect with it. Just as nature allows for many different relative perspectives in spacetime, there can be many different coexisting personal truths for each of us. Let us cherish the fact that we are all different and unique in this way. It seems prudent to encourage, allow, and celebrate the coexistence of such differences when we are able. Rather than feel threatened by the differences of others around us, we can view and embrace them instead as expressions of infinite creativity.

Jumping into the Hole

Being aware of the mysterious nature of black holes seems to elicit more questions than answers. Fundamentally, all of matter that gives us consciousness, existence, and perception is ripped apart once it gets too close to them. How can you possibly define your life without referencing objects made from matter without referencing the passage of time, or the Earth and people around you? It is precisely these things that allow us to declare our existence and express it in some way. So, what happens exactly when spacetime in our universe is affected so strongly and the gravitational pull is so great? Could there be a whole other universe inside of a black hole, another spacetime plane we cannot access from here but where creatures are conscious and experience matter and the passage of time like us? And are we inside of another universe's black hole right now? Or could it be that our universe -- the faraway part that we cannot currently receive signals from -- contains an infinite number of black holes, each of which contain one or more universes with infinite black holes, and so on? The issue of possible absolute reference points for most anything is a very tricky one to try to resolve, because it seems like the more we observe and think, the more apparent it becomes that seemingly basic questions -- not just where or when you are, but how long your life really is or how tall you are -- also cannot be answered in a way that is universally and absolutely true. It might be fair to say we have the illusion of absolutes concerning spacetime because of our experience within the Earth's current natural framework and our human biological makeup. This illusion strengthens the more we all consent to its veracity, but doing so does not make the illusion more or less reflective of the actual conditions nature affords. In the grandest sense, what our universe seems to tell us is that, based on the point of reference, we are both insignificantly tiny and larger than entire universes at once, alive and dead at once, bounded by time and timeless at once. Eternal life and eternal death then both already exist inside each of our passing moments. It may be difficult for our mind to resolve its everyday experience with such things and integrate this knowledge into our sense of sacredness and being. Nonetheless, we can recognize this relativity in nature as an ultimate truth that makes our human experience that much more remarkable.

Once we recognize that any aspect we can bring definition to is actually part of an infinity, that entity becomes all the more sacred and special. Everything you can sense and feel is part of an infinity but experienced finitely by you at the same time. However, much like the friend at the edge of a black hole who experiences all times in a moment, this seeming paradox can be resolved by recognizing each person comes from a different vantage point. Both experience something different, but the fabric of reality allows for their coexistence and resolution. We can explore this general idea a bit further in another way by thinking about different life forms right here on Earth and their perception of time. At one point or another, you may have thought something like "Poor monarch butterflies...their whole lives are just a few weeks!" or something similar. However, how do we know precisely what a day feels like in the experience of the short-lived monarch? From experiments, the experience of time passage for animals with faster metabolism rates appears to slow down compared to us based on their biological makeup. Or what about the oldest known tree dubbed "Methuselah" that is almost 5,000 years old? For that tree, perhaps it has only felt like it has been alive for one of our months? In this way, we can only truly know our own perceived experience, our own look-out point, and nothing and nobody else's. How valuable and respected then should every human life be, and every animal and plant's life?

Everywhere you look around you, there is someone or something that is experiencing an internal landscape that you can never possibly know as fully as your own. This, we could say, is the core of what truly sets us apart from one another -- not clothes, gender, race, age, or job profession -- but our experience of consciousness itself. Take in and recognize that your life, along with the life of every other human and living creature, is its own special independent and infinite universe. Let us honor that, bring awe to that, and carry it with us wherever we go. It is true, you are unique -- just like everybody else. This life, your infinite life and all its intricacies, was made intimately for you.

Chapter 2: Mass and Energy

How Many Things Can You Count?

Go ahead and look at everything in view around you for a moment. How many different, distinguishable objects can you see? Ten? Fifty? If you break some of the objects down into their components, can you challenge yourself to come up with one hundred unique things or more? If you were allowed the chance to pause time and roam the entire Earth, how many different things could you see? On Earth, just the number of discovered species of life stands around 9 million. We might go one level deeper and want to count each distinct person, dog, horse, cat, or cow that looks different from one another to score an even higher number. Once we were done with all the life forms, we could talk about each house, building, street, city, river, and lake. Soon we would be at a number that would rival the number of sand grains on Earth, and we have not even started to count the things out in space. But really, despite our ability to catalog each object and define a difference between them, how many truly different things are out there?

Your body, along with every other detectable object in our universe, is commonly said to have a property called "mass." We usually equate this property with an object's amount of matter, and at its core mass counts the number of fundamental building blocks that are collected together to make up that object. Not too long ago, we believed those fundamental building blocks were atoms, but as we were able to examine atoms more closely, we saw that they too are made up of smaller and more basic building blocks. We now believe there are 61 distinct building block particles we can differentiate between that contribute to the mass and energy of all objects able to absorb or emit electromagnetic radiation. Only 61! Those 61 can be further grouped into just three types due to certain similarities, and there are frameworks to get them all to just one. For the sake of contemplation, however, let us appreciate things with 61. Imagine for a moment you are given the gift of being able to change your size to anything you wanted to while still being able to see and perceive things around you in the same way. You become smaller and smaller until you are on par with the size of these 61 types of building blocks for our universe. In this perspective, everything you could possibly see would look like a confusing dance of just 61 different things: you could see no more. These particles would suddenly pop in and out of existence at different places around you, in a cloudy, nebulous way, and always remain in motion. Perhaps things might appear like a much sped-up video of a fireworks factory explosion, or wisps of vapor flashing and disappearing in all directions. At any rate, this landscape would appear very foreign and confusing compared to our everyday experience. From this vantage point, it would also be impossible to notice how those approximately 10^{80} particles making up the universe are creating the structure and definition of it, as there would be far too many quickly moving objects to keep track of. And worse yet, every time we try to track where one of these particles is located, we lose knowledge about how fast it is moving. To appreciate the number 10^{80}, the number of atoms that make up Earth is about 10^{50}. If we divided up all the visible universe into sections that were about the volume of our body, we would have about 10^{75} pieces. 10^{80} is yet 100,000 times larger than this! Again, despite that gigantic number we are only able to see 61 different things popping in and out of existence at dizzying speeds -- appearing deeply chaotic, but all going somewhere with purpose and direction.

Let us change perspective again and zoom back out to the here and now. Ahh, much calmer by comparison! All the objects you are seeing around you then are not only always in frantic motion on a small scale, but there are still only 61 different possible things working together in a grand and specific way to create those objects. Right now, you have about 10^{28} of these particles coordinating and working in natural harmony to create the mass of your body present at this moment, and much less than the 61 are being used to create your body's mass. In the next instant, the movements change your physical state and allow for your perception of time passage. Every breath you take, every moment you are alive, the particular order you possess rapidly changes and reorganizes. Particles making up carbon dioxide and nitrogen molecules leave your body as new oxygen and nitrogen enter it. Your skin releases water molecule particles into the air as your stomach reorganizes the last food or drink molecules that entered your body. Everything around you that is non-living is also in constant coordinated motion, and its specific collection of mass particles is constantly changing based on its relation to everything surrounding it. The changes and reorganizations might be happening a bit more slowly than those in your body, but they are still progressing nonetheless.

When we take the opposite type of viewpoint and begin to zoom way out from the Earth, first we would see our solar system, then some stars other than our sun, then eventually we would start recognizing the shape of our own spiral-shaped Milky Way galaxy, with Earth sitting about halfway between its center and edge. Zooming out further still, all we start to see are galaxies. Nothing would appear to be moving anymore, and the galaxies would start to look like singular points of light, eternally still. We might begin noticing the structure present between galaxies and ways in which they are clustered throughout the universe. It would look almost completely contradictory in nature to what we witnessed at the smallest scales – instead of frantic movements we would see only calm, motionless, silent points of scattered light. All the dancing would disappear. All the mass of the universe would look like just one static arrangement.

Just like spacetime, we can start to appreciate and recognize that the existence of any object we give definition to is relative and a matter of shared perspective. Fundamentally, the definition rests in the manner we are able to view the size of these collected constituent parts and our awareness of some type of possible difference. While imagining yourself as inconceivably small, think about trying to propose the idea of or trying to define an apple, for instance, at that scale. It would not make any sense because at that size scale the apple cannot be experienced in the way we are familiar with it. As hard as you tried to squint you would not be able to see it. In a similar way, in our everyday experience looking out from our eyes at human scale, it makes little sense to point out a single atom of something to someone -- "Hey, look at that oxygen atom over there!" -- or to try to point out in the sky with your naked eye the details contained in an entire distant galaxy. Though as we change our size scale and perspective, the definition and perception changes to inform and convince us that indeed an oxygen atom is a real and distinguishable player in the dance of matter when viewed by a powerful microscope, and that a galaxy really is an organized collection of billions of distinguishable objects when viewed by a powerful telescope. Not until we zoom in or out does our previous blindness and limitation become far clearer. We are met with one more seeming paradox when it comes to mass, matter, and every object we can conceive of in this universe. It is at the same time a collection of just one or a very small number of fundamental things, or, depending on how we group, divide, and perceive, there exists an infinite way to combine those fundamental things. Just like spacetime, your mass and the mass of everything else you know is a part of the mysterious infinite. It is also bounded by one of the smallest slices of spacetime. Marvel at all of it and make it a practice to feel grateful for each and every object you are able to witness. Take a good look at your very sacred body, your mass, right now. Every part of it is truly part of the infinite, and it will never be quite like it is now ever again.

What Is the Matter with You?

Matter we can see with our eyes is strange enough when we consider it is made of almost countless small building blocks all working together in a very specific way. Beyond this though, what is matter really, and how does it connect back to our idea of spacetime? Imagine watching a moth who is attracted to a lamp left on after it has gotten dark or a fly that appears to be moving aimlessly back and forth around a room that has no way to exit. In either case, we perceive that predicting where the insects are at any given time is impossible. We may try to anticipate and swat while they are in the air, but it is mostly a blind guess. However, while these things are happening, there are a few things we can know with certainty. For instance, the moth will never be found on the moon or any distance that is very far from the lamp for that matter, and the fly trapped in the room will never be found outside of it. We also can say that after any given second they cannot have moved more than a certain distance from their previous spot because of the limitations of their wings. To help describe or predict what is happening in either case, the best we can do is to speak of chances for what can be expected based on what we observe. We can give a higher chance to the moth being closer to the light, though for some reason every so often we will find it further away. The fly, interested in us, is motivated to buzz closer to our heads at any given moment, but may go across the room for a period of time. This is the nature of the small building blocks of matter -- we can never observe where they are located precisely in spacetime, only where they could be next. We could repeat this type of comparison with anything you can imagine that involves chance -- what possibly comes next on a dice roll or what the next card drawn from a deck might be, for example.

If we look at the motion of each building block at any given moment, it may be vibrating back and forth or moving around something else. The speed it is moving may be at or approaching that of a light particle, the fastest known speed allowed in our universe. Like what happens with space and time under strong gravity, as speeds become comparable to the speed of light, the building block's clock runs slower and slower in our perspective. At the speed of light, the experience of space and time passage becomes infinite. If we consider an electron, for example, it moves about one hundredth the speed of light while it is in orbit. According to principles of relativity, for every one of your seconds the electron is experiencing a time passage shorter than this. It will also shrink in size in the spacetime perspective of observers stationary around it. Much like the person standing close to the black hole, each of these building blocks that make up your matter experiences spacetime different than you do. The very things you are built of that allow you to exist are also outside your spacetime perspective at the same time. It is not just the objects around and outside of you that experience infinite variations in spacetime but the objects within you as well. Yet here you are, able to contemplate it all.

There is something else to consider that makes matter very enigmatic. Many objects we see can be described as solid. We could pick up and inspect a chunk of rock and conclude that it is solid, hard, and difficult for anything to pass through it. The only way for you to get through it would be to break it up into the smallest of pieces. When you see something solid, just how solid is it though? How much truly solid space is the object really taking up with its volume? You may be ready to agree that the rock is taking up all the space that is inside its surface, possibly a bit less if small pockets of air found their way inside. Upon breaking the rock in half, we do not see any empty space associated with the make-up of the rock. But when we shrink ourselves down significantly as before, to the point where we can see distances about 1 part in 10 billion of our own height, we find a completely different experience. The building blocks of the rock that are whizzing by us are separated by vast distances. If we consider a simple model of an atom, where the electron building block is moving around a collection of building blocks in its nucleus center, the electron is on average separated from the nucleus by a distance about 10,000 times greater than the size of the nucleus itself. Not to mention the electron size is thought to be about 1,000 times smaller than the nucleus, as well. An imperfect analogy of what is going on would be to imagine a boulder about the size of you sitting in an empty, featureless field. This boulder is made of just a few building blocks, with all of them appearing to be clustered together, in fast motion popping in and out of existence in a certain confined region. Starting at this strange boulder, you walk away in a straight line for 10,000 steps. At this location, at any given moment you are most likely to find a small rock zipping by you, small enough to hold in your hand if it stopped. However, this rock moves so quickly in so many different locations around the boulder that it appears to be many places at once. It is sort of like when you wave your hand back and forth so quickly in front of your face that it appears to be wider than it really is. So, while the small rock is not very big, it does occupy a lot of space in a very short amount of time. While in this strange land, we would certainly not claim that this region is full of rocks or anything else. In the briefest of snapshots, it is overwhelmingly empty, formless space. So, when we say that two things are "touching" each other, for instance, we might imagine no distance between them, but that is always an illusion in a fundamental sense. At any given instant, there will always be mostly empty space separating the things' building blocks, no matter how close we believe we move them in relation to one another.

This is the landscape inside of you and every other "solid" object that you can see. When we zoom in and change our perspective, it seems unreasonable to think that one would even try to claim that the space they were walking around in was completely filled with rocks; rather, it is almost entirely void of them. No matter how solid you think something is -- a beam of steel, a diamond, or even yourself -- upon closer look, there are many aspects about it to suggest a different reality. The idea of something being solid, a liquid, or even gas is one more perception of ours that becomes challenged when we shift our reference frame. And when we zoom out to take the view of all the galaxies, we will also see mostly empty space. It will look like a collection of still points of faint light, though it is really trillions of stars and planets in frantic motion. Just as we would not likely say that our solar system, with vast distances between planets, is completely solid, or that the space of our universe is made up solidly of galaxies, from another point of view that perception could be valid and real.

All There Ever Was, Is, and Will Be

Think for a moment about the last time you misplaced something or searched for something you had seen previously. Why did you look with such conviction? Why in your mind might have you thought, "It *has* to be around here somewhere!"? If you believe you have searched everywhere reasonable and eventually do not find it, you are left to conclude that it is outside the area you are looking, that someone else might have grabbed it, or that it might have been dropped. In an extreme case, maybe it was completely destroyed and might not be able to be recognized anymore. No matter what you believe could have happened, what we would not say is that the stuff the object was made of literally disappeared from existence all together. As far as we know, this is a completely rational and powerful way to get at the nature of what is around us.

As with the above scenario, our mail system, trade system, buildings, money and ability to store things away for tomorrow all ultimately tie back to one central theme we all have come to trust: this is the idea of conservation. We trade money back and forth knowing that we can track it and because there is a limited, countable amount in circulation that passes between all people during any given time. You only mail something because you have confidence that it will be in precisely that same form when the receiver on the other end gets it. We go through the trouble of erecting buildings, roads, water systems, electrical systems, or anything else for that matter because we believe in conservation. We believe it will still be there when we wake up the next morning. If things spontaneously disappeared, really disappeared suddenly, we would not likely even be alive to witness such a system, and the words of this book would not have found you.

On a visible scale, this seems intuitive. We might say that this is ultimately one of the closest universal agreements you will get between all human beings. What happens when we zoom in or out though? When we zoom out to the scale of solar systems or galaxies, we see the planets and stars as pretty stable over time and have come to depend on the stars in the sky to always be there. When we go down to the atomic scale, this also works well. The entire field of chemistry relies on the fact that atoms are conserved. If you put into your atomic mixing bowl 100 atoms of hydrogen and 50 atoms of oxygen, stir it around and see what it turns into, you can count on those same atoms being there, perhaps arranged in a different way, but all accounted for. In our everyday life, all matter we can observe, anything we can define that takes physical form, is to a very high degree extremely stable over time on both large and small scales. However, there is something else to consider if we dig a bit deeper.

All those building blocks that make up your mass stay balanced in a very careful way. Even though they are usually extremely far apart from one another compared to their size, they push and pull on each other (much like the pull of gravity with us and Earth) just enough to keep their interactions going in a cyclic and predictable way. So, we can say, just like in the moth or fly example, where those building blocks might be found at any instant. Looking at mass itself, what ultimately gives the building blocks and particles definition is a mixture of relative movements and pushes and pulls with other spaces. Each building block is a placeholder for describing a collection of moving pushes and pulls. In other words, all matter can be thought of as made from something considered to be even more fundamental to our entire universe: energy. Saying that something has "mass," then, is a type of shortcut to saying that it is a specific collection of tugs, pulls, and movements located inside of a particular spacetime perspective. Mass is a very special type of energy that gives our lives existence and meaning. Pure energy, then, is at the basest level is of what you and everything you see around you consist. Let us take a moment to dwell on that fact a bit. Energy, or moving pushes and pulls, is the only thing that ever was, is, and will be in our universe. Anything else we can possibly imagine traces its origins back to it. And just like perceptions of space and time, energy perception is also relative. Our friend who was subjected to strong gravity, or moving close to the speed of light, will perceive the energy that any given object has as different than you from your perspective. So even energy itself is a relative experience!

It is baffling to think that as complex as the world and universe around us appears, how we can distinguish and define an infinite number of individual things or collections of things, for as much variation of experience there is between any two living creatures or objects, they all become one, not even 61 or three, when we see everything as energy expressions in spacetime. You and I are at our physical core just that. There is nothing underneath this point, and nowhere we can go downward or more fundamental from there. This is what is always expressed across all time and length scales. It is simple, elegant, and beautiful. One of the most powerful laws in science that is counted on time and again, always found to be true without exception, is the conservation of all energy expressions when taken together in an unchanging spacetime perspective. When we consider things like gravity and high speeds of travel, it can never be created or destroyed. Insofar as we can tell, all balances between every single building block and entity in any closed, non-accelerating system obey this law without compromise or question. Everything is always being rebalanced. How amazing is that? Realizing this has allowed us to make reasonable guesses into what unfolded before humans came into existence and to anticipate what may happen in the future. We come to conclusions that we may or may not like, but there is good reason to trust them. It is like flipping through a book with a million pages and knowing that each page will have 100 dots on it, representing energy here, that all look the same. Whether you are on page number 3 or 567,298, the dots can only change location but not their appearance or size. In this sense, we do not know what page of the cosmic book we are on right now, but we do know there are 100 dots on it, just as we believe to know how much energy has always been in our universe. This helps us get at some interesting big questions about things found outside our relative and extremely specific energy spacetime perspective on Earth, like how the stars and planets formed, how life has evolved over time, and what the form of the universe is in the very distant past or future.

Finding Balance

There is a very beautiful and special condition that has been found to occur with forces; that is, when relativistic effects are considered, forces always come in equal and opposite pairs. Every time you push on something, it must push you back just as hard. Right now, as you sit or stand, you are pushing down on some type of surface and that surface pushes right back up on you just as hard in the opposite direction. To get anything to push back against you, you must push on it. Equivalently, if something comes your way and begins the action of pushing on you, you must push on it just as hard in the opposite direction whether you want to or not. These reactions travel through matter at the speed of light. There are everyday examples where this might not seem true. For example, if you grab a rock and throw it, the rock moves forward from your push on it, but you do not move from the push of the rock back on your hand. Why? Whatever ground you would be standing on would keep you from moving back from the friction between your feet and the ground. The ground does not move back because it is connected to Earth which is so massive as to move an imperceptible amount backward. If you threw the same rock while standing on something with almost no friction, like ice, you would start to notice your move backward. After literally thousands of experiments in several different capacities, once relativistic adjustments are made, we find no situation where one force partner is there but pushes back not as hard or is in a direction that is not perfectly opposite.

On a large cosmic scale, on a human scale, and at the atomic building block scale, we see the same conclusion. So not only is our universe made up of conserved moving pushes and pulls, but the pushes and pulls themselves are in balance. The push and the pull between Earth and the moon is in perfect balance. The push and the pull between any two building blocks making up ordinary mass or energy are in perfect balance. No entity can exist, act, or happen without its opposite. To hold your body together in its current form, there are trillions upon trillions of differentiated forces pushing and pulling each other equally to make it happen. This occurs each moment and second of your life that passes. The nature of our universe is to ensure that this balancing act, above all other balancing acts, occurs every smallest fraction of a

45

second for our bodies and every other entity we can observe. The distances involved can be extremely small, like in the nucleus of an atom, or some of the largest we can measure between objects billions of light-years away from each other in space, but our universe does not distinguish between the two. Everything is in a phenomenally, unimaginably delicate and careful balance, with these force pairs rebalancing with precision at the speed of light. Whether we bring focus to this fact or not, our universe takes great care to keep its eternal focus on ensuring this equality.

Think for a moment about the greater implications for something like this. All things we experience derive from this fundamental check and balance. So many higher-level concepts humans have about nature exist only because they have their balanced counterparts. One cannot conceive anything about darkness without having experienced light, cannot understand sound without first knowing silence, or cannot know the sensation of touch without knowing what it is like to not be touched. The entity that is the counterpart can be thought of as the same essence, just in an opposing direction. The same might be said for our emotions; the ecstasy of extreme joy cannot be fully appreciated without having known extreme sadness. One cannot fully know or understand pleasure without pain, peace without discontentment, love without fear, depression without connection, or life without death. It is likely that those around you who know the most about the nature of emotions have been witness to their greatest extremes. Experiences of extreme emotions -- those we deem as either positive or negative -- usually create strong memories and meaning for us in life. Oftentimes it is tempting to desire only the so-called positives in life -- never wanting to be hungry, tired, cold, or sad, for instance. However, we can start to appreciate and accept such things more completely when they are present and while we are experiencing them as we internalize their relation to their counterparts. This is not to say we should intentionally seek out things we might classify as negatives in the human experience, but only when they do come our way, we should embrace, welcome and get to know them for what they are. If you are tired during any moment, fully let yourself feel and know the tiredness, so that you can more deeply understand what it feels like to be full of energy. If you are experiencing physical pain at any moment, be present with it and examine it completely. As the pain changes form, you will be able to know physical pleasure in an ever greater and more fulfilling way. From the very start, all your moments were made to be continually balanced in ways you may recognize as well as ways you may never be able to comprehend.

What Can You See?

It might be reasonable to believe that all the moving, balanced pushes and pulls that the universe contains are ones that we can classify, detect, and observe directly somehow, if only we have some sort of instrument or machine powerful enough. Our day-to-day experience and senses appear to all be physically rooted in and able to be described in terms of some of the fundamental things that have been considered so far -- location, time, mass and energy that we can see from our vantage point. As rare, balanced, and fine-tuned they all have to be to allow for us to be here right now, in recent years we have been learning we are completely blind to many more fundamental pushes and pulls in our universe than we could have ever anticipated. There is something out there that greatly affects our physical reality but operates unseen.

A few decades ago, careful measurements for the motion of distant galaxies were taken, and it was discovered that galaxies further away from us were not only moving faster but were accelerating away at a greater rate. To change the speed of a moving object, there must be some sort of balanced push or pull originating from somewhere and acting in the direction of that acceleration. Wherever we looked, we could not find any energy in the space around these galaxies responsible for creating the pushes or pulls needed to cause this behavior. Furthermore, when we looked more closely inside some of the galaxies, we did not find the amount of mass needed to make them behave in the way they were due to gravitational pulls, even taking into account black holes and all of the known fundamental building blocks making up mass and energy we could directly detect. It may be one thing if it appeared that the mass and energy we were unable to detect was perhaps 1 part in 100, or even 5 or 10 parts in 100. That might tell us that our perceptions are matching reality approximately well, and we just need to do a bit of fine-tuning of our measurement devices to get things to match up more closely. This was not the case, though.

Currently, it is believed that as much as 96%, or 96 parts in 100 of all the moving pushes and pulls in the universe, are "dark." The moving pushes and pulls are further grouped together by describing them as "dark matter" and "dark energy," but the essence of their nature is the same. The word "dark" is used because we can only see their influence but cannot observe them with the best technology we have been able to develop. Dark matter and dark energy have not yet been proven in a traditional sense or directly detected so far. They do not interact at all with electromagnetic radiation such as radio waves and light waves. However, in very real ways this mysterious entity is guiding the behavior of everything we can see on the grandest of cosmic scales.

Concerning dark energy, it is believed to permeate all of space in a uniform way. Dark energy is the energy known to exist in space otherwise thought to be "empty." Perhaps it is the spirit energy for the entire universe? An interesting consequence is that as new space is created, or when the very fabric of spacetime is stretched, new dark energy is also created. So, the total energy of our observable universe increases as this dark energy works to keep accelerating entire galaxies away from each other as our universe continues to expand. As galaxies continue to accelerate away from us, their appearance and speed relative to us in turn also change. However, without this presence of dark energy, long ago gravity may have pulled galaxies into one another, ending in ruthless cosmic violence, and we may not be here at all. In a similar way, if dark matter were not present in the vicinity of galaxies in just the right amounts, galaxies, and in turn planets, would not be able to form in the way that they have. How amazing is it that something we cannot experience with our senses helps keep everything balanced in such a major way?

Both dark energy and dark matter are excellent examples of things in nature that are absolutely critical for our existence but escape the reach of our direct experience. Insofar as we know, no person will ever be able to see or feel them, as they both act as unseen guiding spirits that pass right through the matter we are made of but still have great influence on our lives. Perhaps in the future we will discover yet other elements within spacetime that are necessary for our existence and survival. We should always keep an open mind, recognizing that our picture of how nature behaves is constantly evolving and being updated. It is difficult to tell whether our full picture of the workings of nature at this time in history is closer to a fuzzy black and white or a full color palette with sharp detail. It is important to keep questioning the nature of the reality that surrounds you so that both your own and others' pictures might become clearer. There is always something -- some nugget of wisdom, observation or experience to share -- that you can contribute from your unique point of focus.

Chapter 3: Chaos and Order

Is Chaos Real?

Within our exquisite universe, it seems like the human mind is set up and wired in a way to be able to intuitively recognize things it believes to be chaotic and things in which it finds order. From time to time, one might base how their life is going based on these recognitions and say something like, "This past week my life has been pure chaos!" and then proceed to give some situations when unexpected, undesired, or seemingly random things happened to them during that week. But was that week really chaotic, or was it mostly ordered? An infinite ordered history is behind what unfolds before you during a week. To look at order and chaos in a more basic way, let us take a step back and think about the possible order and chaos for three objects in a straight row spaced equally. The first object is an apple, the second a banana, and the third a carrot. Two people are trying to present their case as to whether there is order amongst these three objects. The first gives several reasons why they say "no;" two are fruits and one is a vegetable, they are different colors, they are different shapes and sizes, two have peels and one does not, two have stems and one does not, they contain different amounts of sugar, they contain different amounts of potassium, two grow on trees and one grows in the ground, two can grow in cooler climates and one requires a hot climate, and one grows in bunches but the other two do not. The second person then provides several reasons why the answer is "yes;" the spacing between them is the same, from the first object to second, and second to third the spacing is in the same straight-line direction, they are all expressions of moving balanced pushes and pulls in spacetime, they are all plant life, they are all edible by humans, the first letters of their names follow the same order as the first three letters of the English alphabet, they were all produced on a farm, we can pick them all up with our hands, and they all contain water. Who is right? It seems like we have bumped up again against the fact that different experiences and vantage points can simultaneously be valid.

Based on these two people's different perceptions, does the nature of the objects themselves change? Is their physical reality of what fundamental building blocks they are made of altered based on how they are perceived? From our particular spacetime vantage point, we can just say that they possess mass. They are just there. Anything that is reasoned past that as to whether they are ordered or not is tied to perceiving a quality of sameness or pattern, or not. Our minds tend to keep a greater level of contentment when we perceive more pattern and order than not, especially when it comes to those things which keep us alive. Most people would agree that they are more content and at peace when the pattern of being able to take their next breath of air at the moment they wish is kept intact, or not getting sick or hurt too often, or being able to go to bed and wake up around the same time each day, or receiving their next meal with relative ease every time they are hungry, or having shelter available each night to help shield themselves from outside animals and extremes in weather, or having continued access to clean running water and electricity. If one or a number of these patterns become disrupted, you or I might begin telling others that our lives are getting more and more chaotic. We might feel like we are losing control over order. Yet at a deeper level, this is not necessarily an absolute truth, but a relative perception. Despite any of these things, as unpleasant as they may be to experience, there is still unimaginable order and rules being kept in check within the building blocks creating you, and an unimaginable order and spacetime infinities in each and every object that is around you as your perceived "chaos" ensues.

It might be said then that, based on our past experiences and what we are able to associate, it is possible to see either order or chaos as we decide to define them. As our awareness grows around the various forms of order and pattern in our universe, it is to our advantage to focus on them to bring our minds back to a place of contentment and trust in the next moment that unfolds. Though if chaos is perceived, we should appreciate it and recognize that its very conception must exist for us to find order. Perceived chaos is always an opportunity whispering to us to find the order within it. A group of several children playing, crowds of people gathered in a busy city, or even the weather system all have massive amounts of order within them. We generally feel enlightened when learning of or discovering new patterns of order. Listening to others from their perspective can teach us so much about the systems of order in the physical, spiritual, and emotional realms we may be overlooking and are oblivious to. But they are there, and the more we look, the more order is found. By examining genetic material found in deoxyribonucleic acid (DNA) more closely, we were able to find pattern and order in the blueprint for life itself. Entire diseases thought to be randomly transmitted from person to person have now been completely eradicated after we discovered the order in the transmission pattern with closer focus. Complex machines, communications systems, and computers all operate because we were able to discover the repeatable patterns and order present in the materials that create them that we were once ignorant of.

At the core of it, chaos and order are ideas mapped out in our minds. What we have found is minds that focus primarily on the idea of order and the ways in which objects, people, and experiences are connected to one another in the spirit of order function in a much healthier and more sustainable way than minds that dwell on constant chaos. Both exist and are equally as real, but it is worthwhile to practice focusing on the existence of pattern and order in your life and in the universe around you to cultivate a healthy and peaceful mind. If you chose to look long enough and persist, you can eventually know and feel deep within you that being able to actively transmute any perceived chaos around you into perceived order is an important benchmark for a life filled with peace, love, connection, and happiness. And if you are ever stuck on how to find the order, you can always draw back to how the nature of everything really is the same -- carefully balanced in spacetime, in constant motion, and fundamentally made of just one thing.

Why Can't You Keep Your Room Clean?

As nature has been examined more closely, we have found ways to physically quantify and define chaos and order present in all collections of mass and energy. We define the amount of order as the amount of information needed to completely define a physical system. Less information needed to define the system means more order. As the information required goes up, so too does the degree of chaos. This same idea also helps establish the direction of time, of cause coming before effect, and how the way the total collection of moving pushes and pulls in all the universe will never be the same again no matter how much time elapses. In other words, it gives credence to the uniqueness of every sliver of time that has ever unfolded. To help further understand this distinction between physical order and chaos, we might think about something that first exists in perfect order, such as ten identical objects placed next to each other at regularly spaced intervals. If left unchecked, nature is set up to encourage that these objects each change into something else such that over time they are no longer identical, and that they will move toward or away from each other at some point and no longer have the same amount of space between them. Their degree of order is decreased, and we need more information to describe how they are now arranged. In the most optimal times, the degree of physical order of these items, if left unchecked, will stay the same but never increase. Over time then, we start to get more differentiation, or we can say a higher degree of physical chaos, amongst the items. We need to look to more and more base quantities before we can again find order. If they do stay in their original form, perfectly preserved, it is because some effort outside of the objects themselves intentionally kept them that way. If you think about this a bit, you should be able to recognize several examples that work just like this on Earth; a giant boulder breaks down into sand over many years unless we protect it from the elements; a surface needs to be repainted because the paint chips unless we keep it in a climate-controlled insulated room; wood rots unless we keep it dry or away from air; fruit ripens and eventually blackens unless we freeze it; and car tires wear away their treads unless we do not drive them.

Everything we perceive around us, even our own bodies as well, work this way. We clean, or order, the objects in a room, and over time it tends to get messy, or more chaotic. We need to dust surfaces frequently to keep them in their original form. We order our relationships with others, and without putting any effort or focus into those relationships, they tend to lose meaning or hold chaos. We do not discipline our minds well enough, and we start eating unhealthy foods or giving up habits that keep us physically, mentally, or spiritually strong. Without putting food, water or oxygen into our bodies, the order our bodies are holding right now quickly decreases. Perhaps this can be very a bit unsettling to think about because it implies two things: that if we pull the arrow of time backward to the earliest moment possible, there was perfect order or sameness within our physical universe; and if we advance the arrow of time forward to the latest moment possible, there will be only emptiness and chaos in the physical realm. The only type of order that will exist at that time is the repeatable featurelessness of spacetime. So, the direction of things may seem like a bit of a downer -- that everything is set up to inevitably go from physical order to chaos, and not progress the other way around. In this grandest, most universal sense, this is true, but there is much more to the story.

What is also important to realize when conceptualizing order and chaos within any entity is that if something's order is increased over time, with the total order of the universe having to go down over time, the only way this is possible is to transfer the order present from one portion of the universe to another. This is happening in real time, all the time. For example, every time we build a dwelling, we bring order to things that were previously disordered. On a deeper level, we might ask where the order for all life on Earth came into being? Where was it transferred from? It turns out that the sun, though millions of degrees hot and extremely far away from us, is set up to transfer all the order needed for each and every life form to exist. The incredible pressure and temperature found inside the sun, along with the presence of specific pushes and pulls within atoms, is enough to transform two hydrogen atoms next to one another into one helium atom, a process known as atomic fusion. This decreases the sun's total order and also emits a light particle as a byproduct. If this light particle is emitted in the direction of Earth, it takes about 500 seconds of travel through the emptiness of space before reaching Earth's surface. This process, and uniquely this process, has generated enough light particles over billions of years that have been used to provide the order in all plant and animal life you observe around you. Without this process, which is literally a continuous stream of transmitted order, we would not be here right now to ponder these things. Everything you eat can trace its origins of order to the sun and acts as a sort of order-storage midpoint for us so that we can maintain our ordered state. How amazing is our sun along with each piece of food we eat from its bounty? The sun has just the right size and sits at a location away from us at just the right distance so that we are given just enough. A little bit more, and it is too hot for the collective of current life forms to exist. A little bit less, and it is too cold.

It can be an amazing experience to look up at the sun and think about how fundamentally important it is to our existence and ability to be conscious in the way that we are. From observing other distant stars and from what we know about the direction of order to chaos, we can say with certitude that eventually the sun will one day have no more light particles to send our way and no more order for us to borrow. Currently, it is estimated that this will not happen for about another 7 or 8 billion years, but it is humbling to recognize that none of what is around us is allowed by nature to be here forever. Even if we hold tight to our Earth's tiny and relative spacetime perspective, it will ultimately disintegrate into nothingness. Our universe will simply not let us hold onto it in its current form indefinitely. From our highly limited perspective, we may observe eternal stability for things like the sun, moon, or Earth, or at least very basic sorts of things like atomic building blocks or the light particles themselves. However, given long enough -- times of trillions upon trillions of years -- all forms of order end. Whatever you can see, touch, smell, or hear around you will eventually decay into the vast darkness of space. The ground below you will no longer be there to stand upon. How awesome is it that you can experience its temporality right now? Pay close attention to this moment because it will never be quite this way again. All moments for all of us, always, are together unique. This is just one more reason to make sure you do not miss it, because it has never been and will never be here again for all times to come.

So, What Do You Do?

The types of order we observe around us will naturally turn into chaos over time, but our minds are focused on creating or maintaining some type of order most of the time. You might not think of yourself as someone who is neat or always wants order around, and you and may even think about how you feel happy when something feels like it turns to chaos around you. Perhaps a storm is an exciting time for you because you like anticipating what the aftermath might look like. Maybe you enjoy seeing a confident sports team you do not like very much believe they have a match under control only to eventually fall short. Or maybe there is a person you despise in political power, and you wish for them to make a big mistake and fall from their rank. Although there are many instances in our lives when we may desire forms of chaos, it is usually at the cost of building order somewhere else. Usually these sorts of desires begin with envisioning a new type of order or pattern we have noticed in the past somewhere and wanting such patterns to continue. Generally, the more we can accurately call out patterns of order we desire before they unfold, the better we feel. How satisfying is it to call something out and then have that thing happen? You might say, "See, I just knew that storm was going to knock down a bunch of trees," or, "I knew that team was being too cocky and it was going to catch up to them. Now, they will have to see the truth of their arrogance and show some humility!" What we really want is a new type of order after the period of chaos. What is not desired within the human condition is perceiving constant chaos around you that never ends, in the sense that you are not experiencing any patterns of importance long enough to help settle your mind. Our minds do not operate effectively when we cannot perceive some semblance of order around us. To have a contented life, it seems necessary to be able to anticipate the unfolding and realization of at least some things important to you. You might not care whether a stranger that walks past you eventually becomes your friend, but you may desire order around the relationship you hold with a close relative or neighbor.

When we examine our own lives, we can start to see ourselves as agents who witness things that we first see as chaos, then after focus and attention bring order to those things. In fact, if you are currently employed or working for yourself, no matter what you happen to do, your job is the same as everybody else's. A job you might have done in the past falls into this as well. All jobs are an effort to bring a perceived order in some capacity to something that previously had a higher level of perceived chaos. You can never go wrong if someone asks you what you want to do with your life in the future, or what you currently do and you answer, "bring a perceived order to a perceived chaos." The world economy operates on this principle, and day-to-day it drives us forward. If we take a step back, it is amazing to see how many ways this can be executed, our differences in perception of order and chaos, and the sheer diversity of jobs people can have bringing order to chaos. One person may be a rural sheepherder, another demolishes buildings, while another heads a 50,000 person company. When we go down one level more and start to realize some of the many ways that all life forms are working to create new and differentiated forms of order, it is simply mind-boggling. A blade of grass waits in the sun and adds to its order from the light particles ending their 500 second journey across space, while an ant places one more grain of sand on the colony's mound. The ways in which humans and other life forms in nature can put their focus and attention into bringing new order seem to be limitless, yet collectively in the grandest sense are still restricted and outmatched by the necessity for greater universal disorder.

Perhaps one of the aspects of greatest importance within your life journey is witnessing the ways in which you bring new forms of order. Whether this takes the form of helping create a new law or policy; making, moving or harvesting a product; constructing a new building; creating a new business; teaching or training others; building teams that focus together on a goal; helping care for someone in need; or making a discovery in medicine; we are all met with a different type of witness. None of us will create order in quite the same way, and we might not agree with the ways others are going about creating order (and might view them as chaos-inducing instead), mostly because our moments of consciousness and being have been a very different experience from theirs. What is important to realize is that all order-creating processes are ultimately important and necessary for what unfolds in every moment. Each aspect, balanced by moving pushes and pulls, is needed to keep the present moment exactly how it is for you to experience. There is no job that can be done without having some previously created order to build upon and move to a new state. In other words, you cannot do what you are doing now unless everyone else has done what they have done.

Scores of people around the world do not describe themselves as happy or content performing their responsibilities. Perhaps you are one of them. There are so many possible reasons for this: they do not like the people they are around, they do not think the work they do is important, commute time and hours are too long, they do not feel a sense of freedom, the work is not interesting, and so forth. Some people, however, absolutely love their responsibilities and find them completely satisfying and fulfilling. Why such a vast difference in attitudes? It seems like in many cases it comes down to whether you feel a sense of control about the outcome or have an interest in the order you create. However, what if you were never in control of outcomes in the first place? What if it is not possible for you to ever realize the importance of what you are doing while you are doing it? Because all moments and spaces are connected to each other in a deep and intimate way, your limited view will always be obscured from fully knowing how your job, your work, your interactions with everyone and everything you encounter, affects everything else. Perhaps you see your responsibilities or accomplishments as a point of pride: *"Everyone see my greatness! I just saved that company a bunch of money!"* Perhaps you do not see what you do as a point of pride at all: *"I just clean hotel rooms most of my waking hours. Anyone can do this, and my job is not very important."* Either way, perhaps it is time to start viewing the matter differently. Maybe saving that company money was not very positive to many people after all, as it put hundreds of employees out of work and stressed their families. Maybe cleaning the hotel room in turn saves someone who you will never meet from contracting a deadly disease that would have taken their life in the next week. Because we cannot directly know all the conditions that led to our ability to create our pocket of order, and because we cannot directly know what that order will lead to one day, week, month, century, or 100 million years from now, we should not be so proud or look to be lauded for whatever we do. What if, instead, when we saw anyone or anything around us creating order, we just appreciated its unfolding and marveled at both the past and future possibilities and conditions needed for that order to be created? Perhaps there are none amongst us who are doing anything any better than another when we take the widest of views. Maybe the perception in difference of importance that we define as a society is only a sort of illusion based on an extremely limited vantage point of awareness. When considering all movement and action as a needed part for nature to do what it does in the next moment, it means that any work you do is just as important and necessary as anyone else's work. Whatever job or work you might be involved in and doing in very real ways is critical, connected, and beautiful to the rest of the world and the universe in ways that defy our imagination.

Chapter 4: Evolution and Devolution

Infinite, Pure Energy

One of the biggest and most challenging questions that can ever be asked is "How exactly did we get to the here and now?" As far as we can tell, we are the only creatures in the entire universe that are able to ask that question. This is a deeply perplexing question that most everyone has asked at some point in their lifetime. At a certain age, you are usually content with hearing that you got here from your parents and grandparents, but as you begin to be able to ponder past that, things get complicated very quickly. There is no shortage of explanations and answers you might find in religious and spiritual texts, and within the framework of science there are several theories, as well. However, an answer which sufficiently captures the grandiosity of the exact path of "how" will always escape us. We can try to guess a bit though based on some of the observations humanity has made about our universe's nature. To try to put together the puzzle, we need to make a bit of a reach and assume that some of the ideas about the nature of reality discussed so far have invariably always been true. For example, we need to assume that the nature of spacetime and the ability to measure distances between things would have been consistent with what we see today compared to, say, ten billion years ago, that the strength of gravity and other pulls and pushes have remained the same, that the sum total of mass and energy have always been conserved inside particular reference frames, that fundamental building blocks we see now have been stable over long periods of time, that pushes and pulls have always been equal and opposite to one another, and that the total amount of chaos in the physical realm has been consistently increasing over time. These things may seem reasonable, but doing this is actually quite a big leap, especially when we consider the earliest moments of our universe. Thinking about how different specific spacetime perspectives can contain relative amounts of fundamental tugs, pulls, and speeds at which things are traveling, we quickly bump up again into an infinite number of ways we might imagine the creation of the universe itself if only we could step outside and observe it from some external vantage point. It is as if we were standing atop a mountain and watching a herd of animals making their way through the terrain. But just like the black hole, we can only guess using things we have observed and assume that certain trends continue over vast distances and times.

As mentioned earlier, not too long-ago measurements were made that indicated galaxies were moving both away from us and increasing their speed over time. The further the galaxy, the faster it was moving *and* the more it was speeding up. This observation led us to the conclusion that there is a dark energy pervading our universe, an unseen energy which is thought to be uniform across all of space and provides the forces needed to keep the galaxies moving the way they are. Alternately, perhaps there are measurements we make at shorter cosmic distances that do not continue in the same linear way that we cannot detect until we get to much larger scales. Maybe, it is a sort of order that is only revealed at large enough scales. Think about if you were trying to determine whether apple trees could grow oranges. You look through one hundred apple trees in an orchard and never see an orange, so you feel certain that apple trees will never grow oranges. Yet, if you could search trillions upon trillions of trees, every billion or so trees you start to find a very tiny baby orange in its branches. As you increase the number of trees you search, you start to collect a significant number of oranges from the apple trees. There is no reason you would ever suspect this possibility, no pattern or order to notice, if the only world you ever knew was the one-hundred tree orchard. So maybe dark energy operates much like this in our universe? The larger point here is there are so many fundamental features in our universe that could possibly operate this way, even popping in and out of existence at different times. We should leave room for this as a possibility. However, using our best methods of observation and inferences about those observations we conclude that since the beginning of the universe, it has been busy expanding and pushing galaxies away from each other. In tandem, each moment of expansion adds more and more dark energy to the universe. If we think of it like a movie in reverse, our measurements point to our universe having a distinct origin as a singular point of infinitely dense pure ordered energy about 13.8 billion years ago, an entity that is responsible for all of nature and our reality.

Commonly referred to as the "Big Bang," this theoretical origin event would have initially been on the smallest of spacetime scales possible (things were not yet "big") and would have created no sound (so no "bang"). We give it this name as a placeholder, but it is impossible for us to imagine what the earliest possible form of the universe would have been like as a singular point containing infinite, pure ordered energy lacking any form of physical chaos. There were no creatures able to exist within this entity because our building blocks for matter would not have been created or stabilized yet. There would be no way of witnessing events or time unfolding, and no space to speak of as spacetime itself would not yet have come into being. Trying to begin imagining these sorts of conditions challenge even the most creative minds. Yet, there is something we can appreciate within this type of mental exercise, and that is the oneness of our ultimate origin. Whatever it was, our deep roots appear to come from the same state of pure energy with its source rife in creativity and artistry. Your body is a child of pure ordered energy, infinite in its potential for expression. We and everything in existence are all children of infinite, purely ordered energy, and we are gifted each moment of our being by its source.

I'm Looking at A Superstar Right Now

During the early moments after the origin, everything is thought to have been at impossibly hot temperatures equivalent to about 10^{32} degrees Celsius, with new, fundamental forms of order being created. The basic building blocks of matter we are made of each have their physical opposites, known as antimatter, and all these particles were very busy forming, finding their opposites, and canceling each other out. On the scope of the entire universe, there is only slightly more matter than antimatter, so if it had turned out the other way, we have nothing to form our galaxies as we see them today, or we would be living in a sort of "antimatter" universe existence. All the fundamental balanced moving pushes and pulls we can observe in the form of mass and energy were being calibrated and the laws of nature were stabilizing the existence of matter. Relative to our vantage point around this unfolding, it could have taken just a few seconds or an eternity. Eventually, the universe cooled down enough so that light particles could exist, and the atomic structure could be realized for hydrogen, helium and lithium, the most basic of atoms in terms of structure. It was still an extremely hot and unstable place, and looking in on something like this would no doubt appear flooded with the brightest of lights everywhere, washing out everything else around you if an eye were there to witness. The very fabric of spacetime and gravity was forming, and the universe, even in those early moments, was making sure that all the tugs and pulls of this seeming chaos were balanced just so. Infinite, pure energy was carefully molding itself into something that would eventually allow us to witness it billions of years later in precisely the way we do.

As space continued to expand, all the atoms floating through spacetime were being pulled in toward each other. Just like the earlier example of people running to the shop to get free gold, each atom was affected by its nearest influence and they started to clump together. Compared to the length of our lifetime, this clumping together took quite some time. It is thought that it took the equivalent of about 100-200 million years before enough atoms were pulled together by gravity to create the first stars. Their spherical shape ensured a new kind of ordering where each atom was as close to the star's center as possible. Next, something happened and is still happening in stars that is very special to the matter we and Earth are made from right now. Remember the process of nuclear fusion happening inside our sun? Only inside of a star do we find high enough temperatures and pressures required to squeeze two hydrogen atoms together to form both a new helium atom (two particles called "neutrons" inside the atom's center compared to just one) and light particles. However, the process does not stop there. Inside a sun's core, if the conditions are just right, fusion between two helium atoms occurs, or fusion between another hydrogen and helium atom occurs, and atoms of beryllium and lithium can be formed, respectively. Once formed, these atoms are very stable, with the balanced tugs and pulls inside their nuclei being the strongest known forces in our universe. Eventually, atoms that have more and more neutrons in their center come into a stable existence. Inside millions and billions of stars, elements such as carbon, nitrogen, oxygen, iron, magnesium, aluminum, and nickel are being formed in proportions that are dependent on those initial conditions of the universe. Everything you see around you and most of the atoms you are made of were at one time deep in the center of a star that was so very far away from where you are right now. These atoms had to make their journey across space through billions of years to be part of you right now. Not one, not one hundred, not even a million of these atoms. We are talking about approximately 10^{27} atoms! To get to that amount it is like gathering up all the grains of sand on Earth, putting them in one spot, and repeating that one billion times.

Just with this fact alone, think for a moment of how specific this is to what you are right now and how everything around you appears. When we start looking at the specific ways that not just your body but everything around you is organized at an atomic level, it defies a complete conceptualization due to the unfathomably large numbers that are involved. Can it be possible that one billion times the amount of sand grains on Earth, by some sort of accident, just happened to create a being capable of appreciating and recognizing this fact? And if despite these large numbers you are still able to consider that it could be an accident, think about how many distinct ways you could arrange that many sand grains. If we talk only about lines (one dimension of space, and not the three dimensions that we exist in), how many ways do you think you could arrange just ten different objects in a line? One hundred different ways? How about one thousand? It turns out that there are more than 3 million ways, and that is just ten objects in one dimension! There are no numbers we have defined that are large enough to describe the different ways your atoms could be rearranged to make something else that is not you. The you that is here right now, with all its supposed flaws, short-comings, and imperfections, is deliberately and precisely how it is supposed to be. We can look to the stars at night and see not just glowing points of faraway light, but places where Earth and its life were literally birthed from. We are intimately connected to stars perhaps more than anything else we can observe in our universe.

After billions of years, if the conditions are just right inside of a star, and it is of sufficient size, it will keep the fusion going to a point where the core starts to cave in on itself due to gravity. If this caving occurs at just the right rate, it initiates an explosive reaction backward that is described as a "supernova." After a supernova, all the transformed atoms shoot outward into space with great energy and in all directions. At this point, it is also possible for a black hole to form, depending on the star's size and mass. Once enough supernovae have occurred in a particular region of space, there is a significant number of dust-like particles, made of all sorts of atoms, floating around. It takes another few billion years before all this dust starts to clump together from gravity and form a critical mass near enough to a star and to be able to make a planet. However improbable this process seems, it is estimated that in our galaxy alone there are about 100 billion of these planets, so in the history of the universe, this has happened several times. Though because each planet is made of unique proportions of different atoms, each with a different mass, there are no two planets that are exactly alike. Our planet just happened to pull together mostly iron, nickel, and magnesium atoms, which the core of the Earth is made of. Only on the thin skin of the Earth, where we have experienced life, do we see the presence of other atoms. Known as the Earth's crust, this special layer is only about 1 part in 1000 the thickness of the entire Earth, and is sometimes compared to the thin skin on an apple. In this outer crust we find mostly oxygen, silicon, aluminum, iron, calcium, sodium, potassium, and magnesium. What is interesting to note is that even among the most common elements in this outer crust, there is very little overlap with the atoms that we are mostly made from. Our bodies are predominantly hydrogen, oxygen, nitrogen, and carbon. So even using Earth as a reference, the very atomic building blocks we are made from are relatively rare. And the story of what it might have taken to get us to the here and now is just getting started.

Setting the Table

From what we can tell through observations of other star sizes, life cycles, and chemical makeups, we can infer that our sun stopped collecting the bulk of its mass about 4.6 billion years ago. It was not one of the earliest stars to be formed. While our sun was coming into existence, the matter needed to put together our Earth was slowly coming together by the pull of gravity. Though to have this matter continually travel around the sun in a cyclic and stable way, two more conditions needed to be there. First, the amount of matter of the Earth had to be less than the matter of the sun -- else the sun would orbit Earth instead. Second, the matter that came from the remains of exploded stars needed not just to be in the right place at the right time, but it also had to be travelling at the right speed. If a chunk of matter were moving too quickly in the vicinity of the sun, gravity would not have a strong enough influence and not enough time to pull it in. That chunk might change its direction of travel a bit and speed up some, but the sun would not be able to pull it in and the chunk would keep moving along away from the sun forever. It is sort of like you not stopping to browse at a shop if you are running past it in a desperate hurry to get somewhere. On the other hand, if the chunk of matter approaches the sun and is moving too slowly, the sun's gravity will pull that piece into it forever. This might be like if you are walking extremely slowly one day, having nothing to do, and seeing a megastore that has more than 100 items you need. However, if the direction and speed the matter is moving at is just right, the sun's pull inward is in perfect balance with what is required to keep it in perpetual motion around it. So, based on Earth's distance from the sun, there is only one possible amount of time it can take the Earth to loop around it once, or what we call a year.

One might imagine that the formation of the Earth was a somewhat gentle process since it took billions of years. However, there was nothing gentle about it. Matter exploded from a supernova is usually travelling at incredibly high speeds, so the early collection of matter that would eventually become Earth was getting bombarded with the space equivalent of super high-speed cannonballs made of molten iron, nickel, and magnesium. Sometimes, the pieces that hit it could be comparable to the size of our planet at that time. Such collisions would have rocked early Earth and changed its speed and therefore orbital distance away from the sun. Earth's surface was extremely hot at this time, made almost entirely of molten rock, no water, and no atmosphere to speak of. At some point, it is theorized that another chunk of matter almost one-third the size of Earth hit it and separated from the Earth enough mass to eventually make our moon. Not surprisingly, the atomic makeup of the moon is very similar to that of the Earth. Another thing important to our daily lives was unfolding as well; as all these chunks hit Earth and the moon, many were hitting off-center, causing them to change the way they spin. In space, once something starts to spin, there is nothing to change its spin unless it gets hit again by an object in space. After the process began to stabilize, the Earth was spinning once around its center about once every 24 hours, what we call a day. It was also spinning about 23.5 degrees different from the direction of its orbital travel, which would pave the way for our change in seasons during the course of a year. The moon was going around the Earth about once every 27.3 days, or what we call a lunar month. Interestingly, this is precisely the same amount of time that it takes the moon to spin around its center once – so the same side of the moon is always facing the Earth. Nobody in the history of humanity has seen the other side of the moon from Earth. Another peculiar aspect was in place, and that is the relationship between the sizes and distances of the Earth, moon, and sun. They are such that at this point in time the size of the moon in the sky and the size of the sun in the sky are approximately the same from our viewpoint, so that on rare occasions when the moon and sun line up we can witness a total solar eclipse. We have found that the moon is very slowly receding away from Earth, so one day this will no longer be possible. Further, several billion years ago the moon would have been much closer to Earth -- so close that it could have taken up about half of the night sky and exerted a much stronger gravitational pull on Earth than it does today. All these aspects were in place long before life got its start on Earth -- everything that our rhythms of life would be molded upon. If these celestial rhythms were changed just a bit, we may not be alive to experience any consciousness at all, or at best it might feel radically different.

It is currently thought that our Earth and moon stabilized about 4.5 billion years ago. Once the Earth ceased being buffeted by so many celestial objects, it could expel more heat back out into space than it was receiving, cooling down the Earth's outer surface. Over time, the cooling allowed incredibly hot steam to reach an energy state just right so it could exist in a liquid state. Just enough space matter in the form of ice had reached Earth so that our oceans could eventually take form. Water pushed its way to the surface due to the fact it was not as dense as the Earth's iron and nickel core. As the relative chaos began to diminish, the thin crust of the Earth and its atmosphere began to order themselves in a new way. Over millions of years the atmosphere formed mainly with carbon dioxide, a bit of water vapor, but almost no oxygen, bearing little resemblance to the atmosphere we see today. The water on the Earth helped cool the molten iron, nickel and magnesium pushing up onto Earth's surface so that it could exist in solid form and help make land. Everything in existence at that time was not alive in the sense we speak of life but still wholly dependent on all the moments that came before it due to the coalescence and harmony around the sum total of nature's moving, balanced tugs and pulls.

At least 3.5 billion years ago, or perhaps longer, another very special and magical event took place on Earth. Deep within the oceans, beyond the reaches of the sun's rays, the earliest known ancestral life form believed to be life's last universal common ancestor (LUCA), entered existence. LUCA had precursive features to both bacteria and archaea but is not classified as either. LUCA found refuge near what are known as hydrothermal vents -- places where hot gases from Earth's core meet the ocean water -- and used the heat energy from these vents to create their order. At some level, they were conscious of other LUCA nearby, the space they were occupying, and how to borrow the ordered heat energy that surrounded them. We would not recognize these creatures today even if we were looking right at them. They typically were about one-tenth the width of a human hair. However small, they are remarkable for several reasons. They are some of the very first known creatures to contain the blueprint for life, or DNA. DNA is known to be a critical and essential aspect for all of life, as it is a complex spiral molecule made of just a few different types of atoms: namely, carbon, hydrogen, oxygen, nitrogen, and phosphorus. To form, it needs to have just the right proportions of these atoms forged deep within exploded stars to come into proximity with each other. The mechanism of how to create just one DNA molecule starting with just those atoms in a different configuration is largely unknown, and if coming to know this mechanism will likely require a very specific process and extremely fine-tuned physical conditions. However it happened, it is possible that the very first creation of a DNA molecule did not first occur on Earth. We will likely never know where it first occurred, as we have discovered numerous asteroids and floating debris in space that contain some of the earliest building blocks for life and precursors needed for DNA. How did they first get there, and what was the purpose of this particular order? It may remain a mystery forever, but however it happened, this pure infinite energy took quite some time and care to ensure that DNA and LUCA would eventually unfold into existence. DNA along with life itself have the unique quality of being set up for a sort of conscious replication, almost always with perfection but sometimes not. It is like the ultimate recipe book guiding you in exquisite detail on how to make a perfect meal, most every time. There is one more thing remarkable about LUCA and its DNA. Through much effort looking at the DNA of ourselves, other species alive today, and fossilized species, it has become clear that all those DNA sets can trace their roots back to LUCA. We can think of it as the one origin to the millions and perhaps billions of life forms this earth has ever seen. Our ultimate mother, this amazing creature had conditions around it that were just right for life to not only replicate but continue to add layers of more complex physical order and pattern around it.

How humbling is it to think that we would not be here had it not been for an ancient creature we cannot even see, who lives in places we would probably never even think to visit? The future potential of this creature was not yet revealed more than 3 billion years ago, and it must have been blind to the influence it would have on the future of life itself. For several million years, it would go on borrowing its order from the Earth's heat, replicating and multiplying itself trillions of times over. Why would it go through that trouble? What was it ultimately trying to do or become? Unfortunately, it is not a question that we could ever ask such a creature, but the answer for LUCA should ultimately be the same answer for us.

Much of the mystery of life, its creation and evolution of new types of order, comes back to the natural tendency for decreasing the order of any particular life form. Using LUCA as an example, let us imagine that conditions were just right for a single organism to first come into existence. Even its supposed "simple" structure, compared to more complex life forms that followed, is not so atomically simple. There are at least thousands of atoms all working in coordination and in a special type of order for this organism to function. So only with the right atomic conditions, one is suddenly brought into existence. Other conditions would not allow it. Why or how is the first one created such that it knows how to make a replica of itself, and that it should keep replicating itself? Yet while it is busy replicating itself, nature is also busy working to dismantle its complex system and change it into something that is ordered in any other way than what it is. But it keeps on borrowing order from something else to sustain its existence.

Why were the conditions of the universe, developing continuously for 10 billion years or so before our LUCA, so specific as to allow its creation, however it happened, at all? Such questions are deeply mystifying, and the same questions extend to all forms of life across all times. Why does it go through the trouble of fighting to exist against all odds, but through existence demonstrates perfect odds so it can set the table and pave the way for us? There are infinite ways that life could have completely perished along the way, though it is here today in a countable form. It seems like one more place where the finite and infinite come together as one.

The Less Than One Percent

As our LUCA was busy striving for existence and multiplying deep in the oceans, the solid crust of the Earth continued to cool and shift around above the hot molten rock beneath the surface, much like a boat gently drifting on a lake. What is known as "strata," or distinct layers of rock, were forming, being added to, and preserving the physical conditions around their formation. Inside some of the strata or between them, we find fossilized remains. These strata are extremely important to us as they contain clues and information about what was alive on Earth at different time periods as well as atmospheric and thermic conditions. Once a new stratum forms, its weight presses down on the previous one and keeps it from further interacting with the outside atmosphere, helping preserve its order over time. If this had not happened, we would likely be much more in the dark about the specifics of Earth's past life.

According to fossil records, around 3 billion years ago bacteria that had evolved in the oceans had developed a process crucial to our existence today, and that is of photosynthesis, or the ability to borrow the order from light particles coming from the sun. This process is magnificent on many levels. During photosynthesis, both water molecules and carbon dioxide molecules from the atmosphere are broken apart and used in such a way that the bacteria get more available energy to continue replicating, and a byproduct of this process just happens to be oxygen gas. Keep in mind that at this time there were no creatures on the Earth for which oxygen in the atmosphere was useful, so it acted as a toxin to them. The moon was still much closer to the Earth than it is today, and its gravity was creating large ocean waves that mixed and transported these bacteria across the globe. Photosynthesis is also magnificent because it uses light particles, which do not experience time from our vantage point, to give order to creatures that do exist in time. It is one of the ultimate crossovers between relative existences. As mentioned earlier, as something gets closer and closer to the speed of light, in its experience time slows down more and more. When something is travelling at exactly the speed of light, it does not age inside of our universe at all. From our perspective, the particle is in motion, but if you were able to take a ride on top of one, you could not experience any events unfolding or any time passing -- you would be eternal. How strange is it to think that the light we see around us is in a very real way part of an infinite existence outside of time, experiencing no beginning or end of it? Bacteria's ability to be the first to harness this part of the infinite to drive life to more complex layers of order is simply astonishing!

There have been several hundred volumes written about the detail of Earth's history of life, and still we continue to find out more and more about it. Each progression and new life form found its own temporary balance between itself and its surroundings, only to have those surroundings continuously shift and change. Everything needed to be just right, with organisms gaining more and more levels of interdependent order, and feeding off one another. Creatures that did not have the capacity for photosynthesis began using the order arising from it for their own existence by digesting it, as we do today. There were so many amazing capabilities that developed before any humans existed on the Earth. It was only 1.2 billion years ago that there was any gender differentiation between members of a species, and the ability to sexually reproduce. This ability greatly increased the genetic diversity found within a given species and created an entirely new order of coexistence. Before this time, all organisms had just a single gender. 600 million years ago saw the first creation of the ozone layer, an extremely thin gaseous layer in our upper atmosphere derived from billions of years of oxygen production from life on Earth. Without this layer, harmful ultraviolet radiation from the sun would get through and wreak havoc on many of the lifeforms in existence today, including us. Life in the water would grow and grow in complexity and form. Eventually, plants and something resembling a fish would make their way onto land, and footprints on land would appear about 530 million years ago. Over time, gills transformed into lungs for oxygen; fins became arms and legs. The entire system and web of life would become more and more interdependent, creating an impossible diversity of creatures completely dependent on the conditions around them in their moments of life to carry them forward and reproduce into the next. Plants, insects, bacteria, viruses, and so many different animals would pop into and out of existence based on the available order they were able to borrow from their surroundings using specific manipulations and abilities written into the instructions encoded in their DNA. Each would sense and be conscious of the world in different ways, whether by looking through an eye to sense objects great distances away, sensing contact through nerves which first also helped propel an organism forward, or sensing vibration through an ear or other appendage. All life forms that would ever live would have a unique and differentiated experience, just like us. Sometimes there were short time periods with quick bursts of greater and greater orders of physical complexity, and sometimes life forms would seem relatively unchanged and consistent by contrast.

This evolution of life did not come without its hardship and trials. From looking at strata, we know that over the last 500 million years there have been five major mass extinctions on Earth where more than 75% of all species completely perished over a geologically short period of time, along with many smaller extinction events. The causes triggering each of these extinction events are not for certain, but were likely due to such things as changes of oxygen levels in the oceans, volcanic eruptions, sudden changes to the Earth's atmospheric make-up, large land masses separating from each other, and large meteorite impacts from space. There were many periods where a sort of mass devolution took place, and the more complex systems of order were wiped out completely. So many species have lived on this earth before us: it is estimated that more than 99% of all species that have ever lived on Earth are no longer in existence. This alone speaks to the incredibly unusual and relative rarity of the plant and animal life that is seen around us today. It is challenging to think of what life on Earth might have been like 300 million years ago or even much less. One thing is clear from Earth's history though: certain levels of organized complexity are more tolerant to changing conditions of the Earth and their surrounding environments, while others are much more delicate. A countless number of creatures, all developing and reacting to conditions around them they inherited but did not create, were striving toward replicating and expanding on ways they could create order around them. Even after the major setbacks, the spirit of life would push on, undeterred, like a mountain climber who might slip on the rocks, bloodied, but gets back up in hopes of reaching the summit. We are amidst the less than one percent: fragile, but beautiful and complex products of billions of years' worth of very determined life forms interacting in one glorious symphony.

How Is Your Family?

One way to visualize what our LUCA and other primal species are to the rest of life is to consider a tree. Our LUCA would be like the seed, containing the capacity for a thick trunk, branches, and leaves, but only realizing that capacity if it has continued access to things like soil, water, sun and an absence of other life eating it. It grows for a bit having a thin vertical trunk, but this quickly splits and there are new branches created. Each branch is an offshoot either from the trunk or from an existing branch. The longer the tree grows and the taller it gets, to get from the end of one branch to the end of another, one must travel a greater and greater distance if you are to cling to the tree at all times. This is very much what it is like when trying to imagine how we are related to, say, monkeys or a blade of grass. Both monkeys and humans are currently at the end of a branch right now, but that branch split not too far back. If we go to where the branch split, we will find our last common ancestor not alive today, which would be neither a monkey or a human but have some traits and systems of both. For us to think of how we are related to a grass blade, we must go back very close to the trunk of the tree where two major branches split from each other to find an ancient ancestor that when it developed in one environment it became a grass blade, but in another environment went through a much different chain of changes over time to eventually become us. The precise mechanisms for how these changes occurred is still very mysterious and debated, with some claiming that different non-living atoms can spontaneously and randomly arrange to inform these changes, and others claiming that a force outside of nature's apparent realm acting with intention and purpose is responsible for the changes. Independent of how each jump or change occurred, we know that it did happen, and in the scope of our own lifetimes it happened extremely slowly.

After the last major extinction around 66 million years ago, a vast diversity of creatures got their start on Earth -- penguins, birds, whales, crocodiles, armadillos, camels, butterflies, deer, giraffes, coyotes, bears, elephants, and several species of primates. Some of those primates would eventually become modern-day humans. Through genetic testing of DNA for millions of people alive today, we are getting a more detailed picture of our relatively recent human history. Using the tree and branch analogy, what we have found for certain is that all females alive today all have one common grandmother thousands of greats over who likely lived in present-day eastern Africa around 150,000 years ago. She sits as the one common seed for every female alive on Earth today, with the tree branches fanning out more and more over time. For males, there is also one common grandfather who also lived around the same time frame in the same region. He sits as the one common seed for every male alive on Earth today. What is not accurate is to say that they were the first humans who appear in the fossil record about 300,000 years ago, or that other humans did not coexist with them when they were alive. So, we also have ancestors who were alive during their time, but such ancestors are just not common to all humans alive today. Whatever the circumstances, the life spirits of our common grandmother and grandfather were the ones that survived through thousands of human generations, while others were eventually not able to reproduce given their surroundings and circumstances. So, in a very real way, we are all family descended from most probably a woman and man who lived in a region in modern-day Africa. Over that amount of time, humans have changed and adapted to their environments quite a bit, such as becoming shorter when living in areas with less available food and changing skin color to help regulate the effects of the sun's rays on the body based on how close they were to the equator. Whatever changes in skin color have occurred in the last 150,000 years have been products of what was physically available and conditions present around the time of each generation. Since that time, many humans have moved out of the region that is modern-day Africa and settled so many varied corners of the world that contain a wide range of food sources and weather conditions. How crazy is it that today many think either more or less of themselves based entirely on adaptive changes that occurred over several thousand years to help ensure their survival? All changes that happened since that time were magnificent and important in continuing to keep our species diversified and resilient. No change was in an absolute way better than the other, only different. All your physical aspects, whether it is your hair or eye color, skin color, height, nose size, or foot size, were all inherited from your surroundings and the surroundings of your ancestors. You are exactly as you are because all of your ancestors -- pre-humans included -- needed to be exactly the way they were to both exist in their environments and reproduce so that you could eventually experience your gift of life in the way you do.

If you have thought in the past that you do not much like your body, take a moment to inspect it thoroughly and realize that you are looking at billions of years of both evolution and devolution. Not your body with makeup, clothes, physical alterations, or accessories, but your body completely stripped down of everything as you were born. Look at everything, including places you might typically not, like the bottom of your feet, your armpit, and lower back. Notice each hair, shape and fold on your face in the mirror. You are looking at not only ancient stars and a vastly empty amount of space, but the result of millions upon millions of interactions between creatures no longer in existence who were predators and prey, and the result of thousands of generations of humans surviving conditions much different from our present-day life. Every curve in your skin, every organ in your body, every feature in your face is a perfect reflection of pure energy manifesting itself over billions of years, of moving balanced pushes and pulls in a long-form dance complex beyond imagination. You are just the way you need to be right now, with all your perceived problems, successes, desires, fears, likes, aches, pains, pleasures, and thoughts. You are right here where you need to be. Do not waste any more time disliking this body or mind that you have in this present moment. Do not compromise doing something as important as that. Love every tiny aspect of your body, how it reacts and compensates, and what it can and cannot do. Each and every day consider the magnificence of how your body has so many different systems all working together in inconceivable ways, and how it allows you to get one next breath, one more heartbeat, one more blink of your eyes. You are finely tuned for life, with the ability to think, feel, and experience connections to all of which is around you. You are an embodiment of life striving toward new and different forms of order, gaining new universally unique awareness and adventures along the way. Keep this truth close to your heart: you, my friend, precisely in your current form and as you are, are nothing short of a glorious, beautiful, wonderful, absolute miracle.

Chapter 5: The Individual and The Collective

What's Most Important to You?

When thinking of the concept of evolution, it is perhaps tempting and easy to think of its process as over time producing "better" organisms that are more "advanced" because they have capabilities unlike their constituent parts or that which came before them. It seems reasonable to marvel more at a giraffe -- its complex patterns on its fur, its ability to run and eat from high in the trees -- than say the more primitive, microscopic and unseen bacteria organisms in its gut that allow for it to break down what it eats and convert it into useful energy and excrement. What metric, though, really causes us to define the giraffe itself as a better expression of life than its gut bacteria, for instance? Is it because giraffes are more easily seen with our eyes? Is it because they can run, and the bacteria cannot? Is it because we see more resemblance to ourselves in the giraffe than the bacteria? What is it about greater degrees of coordinated order that make them more important than their subsystems? Is it a recognition of their fragility as they have a greater tendency to disorder over time? We spend our lives making new types of order from constituent parts, as does all of life, so why this drive to do it? Whatever the reason, it often causes us to overlook holonic relationships, or hierarchies between entities that can be seen in two different directions.

To help understand the idea of holons, consider a house made from bricks, cement, wood, and windows. To get to the idea of "house," we need to arrange these objects together in a certain way. First, we may create a foundation with the cement. Then, we lay the bricks on it and hold them together with more cement. Next, wood is put in place to create the walls and roof, and finally the windows are put in around the bricks. If we are asked to define a hierarchy here, we might think about the steps that occur during the building process. We could say the cement that creates the foundation is at the bottom of the hierarchy, followed by the bricks, the cement that holds the bricks together, then the wood, and finally the windows and roof. Together, they create the top of the hierarchy which is the house. However, what if instead of imagining a hierarchy in this way, we reasoned through it in the opposite direction? What if we saw instead the house as being on the bottom? The reason we now put it on the bottom is because it is the weakest entity in terms of its staying power. If a hurricane or tornado comes along, something on the house changes form -- windows break, the roof is damaged or blown off, or the brick walls give way. Even if this does not happen, over time the roof sags, the bricks shift, or the wood rots. Going to the next levels up we would define the hierarchy this way: bricks are higher than the house, but the clay the bricks are made from is even higher. The clay itself can exist for perhaps millions and even billions more years. And what about the atoms that make the clay? They can go even longer, and the building blocks of the atoms longer still. After this, the highest orders are the moving, balanced pushes and pulls themselves, and at the very top is the pure infinite ordered energy that came before that. So, depending on your perspective, the house can either be at the top of the chain or at the very bottom. There is really nothing to prevent us thinking about it at either extreme, and we can be correct to reason in both directions. Because the house is custom-made and provides warmth and shelter, it is the "whole," and better and more desirable to us than its constituent parts. Even though it can fall, its ability to stay standing in this moment is much more important to us in our relatively short time on Earth than the ability of the atoms to exist well beyond our lifetime. But wait: without pure energy, which is also a "whole" along with the atoms, there is no part of it manifested as a house to even speak of! So that supersedes everything. Looking at this pure energy as the entity at the top of the hierarchy can be thought of as what major religions and those of a spiritual mindset try to embrace.

We can extend this type of thinking to almost any system of order we can observe, including our own bodies. It appears that eventually you must conclude that, much like the infinite possibilities within spacetime experiences, there are infinite possibilities to define different hierarchies. It is then not possible to say that any one entity is better than another in some sort of absolute way. Even when you decide on a fixed metric, say, entities within your body that allow it to sustain life, it is tough going. We might say that because it allows us to think and control our bodies, our brains are the most important organ in our body. Without our heart or lungs though, there is no brain to keep conscious. Similarly, without neurons or blood, there is no brain, so those might be the real sustainers of life. The same can be thought for organ tissue. Perhaps our digestive system and liver are the most important -- after all, they inhibit toxins from entering our system and provide us much needed energy moment to moment. Without these, we would surely die in short order. We can go on playing this sort of mental game indefinitely until we recognize the equal importance of the simultaneous totality of everything that makes up our bodies, and realize that everything all draws on and creates function and meaning from everything else. Yet, we realize that the whole has a quality very different from a simple summation of its parts. Our human experience cannot be fully captured just from adding the experience of our lungs, legs, arms, brain, and heart separately together. There are so many unique human qualities that are completely ignored and reduced if we say, "we're just a collection of atoms." When we put them together, we realize a new form of consciousness that cannot be captured by any of its parts alone. This is the mystery of holons -- all parts are of equal importance to the being of its whole. Further, the very idea of what constitutes the whole and what constitutes the parts is relative. Everything about your being, therefore, is necessary and each part at once equally important as all the rest. This extends to your experiences each moment, your supposed victories and defeats in life, your supposed high and low moments, and your supposed blessings and curses. They are all important to your being and the being of everything and everyone around you in a finely tuned and balanced way. Love and appreciate all of it -- it is all equally good.

Who Do You Work For?

Based on our outlook, we can look in on ourselves as both "one" or "many." You are the collective of all your constituent atoms from a physical level, but they are so small and seemingly insignificant that your body would continue to function as normal if just one of those atoms were missing. In fact, our bodies are shedding hair and skin cells frequently, not to mention everything we excrete from our skin and nether regions. We put new atoms into our body whenever we eat or drink, so where exactly is this individual person that exists inside of us located? We certainly carry the idea of our being one special collective, receiving one name, one age, and one weight at any given time. Using the idea of holons does not necessarily help get us to an understanding of what it is that defines us physically as a person. Yes, simultaneously every atom of your body is important in creating you exactly how you exist in this moment, but in future moments what can change or be removed and still have it be "you"? Certainly, several people have undergone amputations and never get a name change. They continue to interact and remain conscious in much the same way as before. Several people have had kidney, liver, lung, and heart transplants -- entire organs that were not in their bodies before -- but we do not say that their identity is different. And what about people who sustain brain injuries, dementia, or are in comas? Some might say those sorts of things really change who they know the person to be, yet they have more of the same atoms in their bodies than the person who had an organ transplant. Or, how about people who are manic-depressives, extremely bouncy and energetic one moment and cannot get out of bed the next? Who, then, is that person really?

At its core, it seems difficult to presume that our conscious experience or "you" should be considered a singular thing, or that it can, for instance, be adequately captured in static pages of a book or a resume, or even in a set of character traits. Because the collective of what you describe as "you" is a constantly changing effect due to the cause of its environment, its form is perpetually different. It may have shown some patterns of certain order over time, like reporting to the same job for five years, but there is no reason you know of why those patterns must continue. One of the unhealthiest mistakes people can make is to hold tightly onto a way they were in the past, or to obsess about a way they need to be in the future. Who and what you are in all future moments is already taken care of -- there is no need to worry about it if you trust that the grand balancing act will continue as it has in moments past. We tend to classify people as "good" or "bad," or "daring" or "shy," but they are all just doing things that they must do in each and every moment based on the conditions they have inherited just before that point. So, whatever you have been, what you are, and what you will become is all part of great mystery, wonder and excitement. Embrace it as you observe it unfolding. But you are never just one thing, one personality, one consciousness, but many. And within this, you continue to experience unique, diverse, and relative perceptions of spacetime. To pinpoint what it is that constitutes the "you" that both your consciousness and other living organisms' consciousness experience from their perspective is impossible to capture completely.

Consider that there are about 30 trillion or so cells with human DNA in your body alive right now, along with another more than 30 trillion or so bacterial cells in your body that do not contain human DNA. This means that your body has more than 7,000 times the amount of live interacting cells than the world has people. Though it is estimated that more than half of all your body's cells are more ancient in origin and non-human, without them we could not exist in our present form. They are each individually alive, with the human and non-human cells colonizing certain regions, exchanging much needed resources between each other like a perfectly functioning economy. Some are alive for longer than others, and some types, like red blood cells, are more numerous than others. When there is a crisis or invasion of your body, if the cells are able to they rush to the place to help repair it and fight off enemies they know might later weaken or completely disrupt the careful balance that has been established in a way that would end the life of all cells. Imagine for a moment if you were able to shrink yourself to the size of these cells and see them doing what they do, going where they go, birthing new cells, and casting away the ones that perished. This would be one amazing vantage point. If you could stop to talk with one, what might you ask it? You might want to know how it is aware of what it needs to do, why it decided to go through the trouble of making ten new cells and not just one, or why after some time it decided to suddenly stop using the resources around it and perish. And how do they together decide who gets to live and die? You might want to know what it believes its purpose is and its meaning in life. And why is it they believe what they do? Do they see themselves as true individuals or as a part of a team as they operate from their limited perspective? Who do they decide is on their team? The cell may not know how to answer these things, but they are curious questions nevertheless.

As our higher-order human consciousness depends on all of these collective decisions or compulsions of cells working in harmony, however we wish to imagine them, we are generally grateful for the outcome of their continuously prolonging our life through our next breath or heartbeat. There are so many individual cells that are born into existence and die inside our bodies during our lifetime to create what is thought of as our one human life. In fact, about 100 billion cells will die in your body just today, and each year your body will cast away and replace enough cells to equal your body mass. It might be argued that you live only because of the sacrifice, focus, diligence, and determination of cells all working to keep you conscious. Now, let us reimagine this scenario with a different type of "body" that exists when we zoom out a bit. This new type of entity, instead of having trillions of different cells working together, has just 7 or 8 billion individual humans as its distinct entities. We refer to it as humankind. In this perspective, the one humankind, just like your body, is in a constant state of exchange and trade of goods, services, and information. Imagine if a being that was conscious at the level of the entirety of humankind, a consciousness not able to be captured by any one human element, were to be able to shrink down and ask us some of the same questions that we wanted to ask our cells. They might ask some of the same things. For us, it is perfectly acceptable that all our cells are born and die when they do if it is needed to keep us alive. But if the organism is humankind, it can start to feel like maybe it is unfair that we happen to be the cell whose turn it is to get injured or die. We might feel like it is unfair doing the work that we do, feeling the things we feel, or not being as healthy or having as much money as the other cells around us. Unless we dig into the billions of years of history leading up to the present moment, a sense of fairness and balance will never make sense, but our universe has never lost track. We must recognize that much like our human cells working in harmony with our body's non-human cells to create a greater order, so too must we ensure that we work in harmony with the non-human living world to maintain our health, and accept our purpose and fleeting existence in a way that is healthy.

Just like the cells in our body, sometimes we happen to be amongst those that can be a bit more passive -- relaxed, calm, without a worry in the world. Sometimes though, we are called to react and protect not just our own lives, but the lives and health of those around us in ways we are immediately able. Just like in our body, sometimes the best way to do that is to send a signal to someone far beyond our physical reach, so that they can act on our urging. Many times, we are the receiver of signals from others, as well. Seen in this way, our communication systems, cities, roads, and countries can take on different meanings. What other cells are we working in harmony with, and how are we communicating with those cells to add different orders of awareness and health to the larger humankind and life body? For better or for worse, our function is to exist as a single cell within the larger organism for a relatively short amount of time, during which we are of service to it in some way and either add new cells to the organism or not. Every cell has its unique purpose and is just important as the next, though. Some cells will be relatively stationary their whole lives and only know the experience of those immediately surrounding them, while some cells are transporters and cycle through the larger body with great frequency. Though differentiated, every cell that is added or removed changes the nature, ability, and essence of the larger humankind organism. You and I are both cells serving beautiful and unique functions to create something much larger than either one of us. How amazing is it that we are all part of the same magnificent single human organism?

What Do You Do to Stay Healthy?

For any living organism we can see with the naked eye, its life-sustaining function is dependent on the collective health of its individual cells. If an organism has a million cells and just one of them is unhealthy, things tend to progress in one of two ways. The first is that the healthy cells around it are able to give it more resources and nutrients it needs, and it becomes healthy again, or it dies off and is replaced by another healthy cell. The second is that the unhealthy cell is allowed to replicate or takes resources from area cells that will in turn begin to have them compromise their function. The balance between the healthy and unhealthy cells determines both the quality of the organism's life, and whether it gets one more moment to live. It is a careful, fine balance between how many unhealthy cells there are compared to the healthy ones before the unhealthy ones win out and eventually kill an organism. Because each organism is a bit different with a history and environment that are unique, it is impossible to determine an outcome in advance with complete accuracy. Think about how many times doctors have told people that, based on their condition, they have just a month to live and end up living another two decades, or how often someone who appears totally healthy suddenly passes away in their sleep. You may even have had an experience where you thought for a moment there was a good chance that you were going to die and did not.

The condition upon which an organism continues to function is when its cellular structure works together in a specific way to create the order needed to maintain the organism's life. Over time, we have discovered several ways that organisms become compromised or diseased: for example, by a parasite that lives inside of the organism and takes a significant amount of its order, or a cancer that is allowed to grow bigger and bigger without the body's immune system recognizing it, or a virus that enters the body and replicates quickly before the body knows how to get rid of it. Anything we refer to as a "disease" is literally just that: anything that creates dis-ease for the organism or prevents it from existing in a peaceful way. Though our own bodies are incredibly fine-tuned with immune systems, complex beyond full comprehension, to fight off disease every second of our existence, the system is not created in such a way that it is limitless in its capacity. If it were, the balance needed between all life forms would not be what it is. However, if we want to keep our immune systems as strong as they can be and perform as they were designed, we have uncovered some conditions that encourage this. We have found that positive internal dialog with ourselves, goal setting, and being generous with others encourages immune system health. Certain amounts of sleep at regular intervals ensure our brains can reset and clear away many of the disordered fluids they created during waking hours. Sleep also ensures cells have time to repair themselves among many other things that recalibrate to encourage good immunity. We have learned that certain substances can act as toxins to our system, sapping a lot of attention and energy from our immune system when we put them inside our body. Our immune system has only so much action it is able to do, so every time we knowingly or unknowingly put toxins into our bodies, the system allocates its resources to handle these and can overlook something it is otherwise able to fight off. It is like a fire department that has only ten members. They all get dispatched to take care of ten small fires, only to have a larger fire engulf the town center they cannot then reach in time. Things like alcohol, processed foods, inhaled smoke or vapor, high amounts of sugar, and a sedentary lifestyle can all act as toxins our immune systems must continually work against to maintain our body's order. Things like fresh foods closest to their raw forms, eating a variety of foods, as well as moderate levels of physical exercise throughout the day are all known to help assist most immune systems and allow them a more peaceful existence by comparison.

Under environmental conditions favorable to our immune system, we find that the system is able to be at its most alert, efficient and conscious state. At its best, it possesses the awareness to fight off the greatest number of threats— whether of physical or psychological origin -- that could possibly reduce in quality or end our lives. When the conditions around the immune system cells and organs are such that they are at peace with their surroundings, or without disease, they are in turn able to provide the larger organism that peace. It is truly a system of symbiosis and balance that we have with our immune systems -- we help provide it things that encourage its peace and allow it to be alert, and in turn it is allowed to do the same for our being. Now let us consider ourselves again as cells within the larger organism of humanity. In a similar way, if we seek to maintain peace and a sense of readiness, ready to assist in the peace and readiness of those around us, then we allow the human organism to gain both a greater sense of consciousness and peace within itself. If we are very fortunate, we will have had others around us at peace and helping us to maintain ours. If you were at the seat of consciousness for the larger human organism, just like our cells struggle to the best of their ability to be at peace and ready to act when needed, this organism expects this struggle from us too, if its health is to be maintained and optimized.

It is for this reason it is important to make a priority, above all else, to maintain your physical, social, emotional, spiritual and other forms of health that your body and mind, with billions of years of evolutionary history reacting to environments, has knowledge of. Just like a single cell in a larger organism, if you are not prioritizing a maintenance of this health, you might die off yourself, or else survive while spreading an unhealthy way of being to others as an example. Living and being with healthy habits is not only helpful for you but influences those around you, children and adults alike, potentially for generations. A trap that some can fall into is mistakenly thinking they must extend and tire themselves while in the service of others to a point of exhaustion or resentment of the service itself. This is not healthy for the human organism, as ways of peaceful being are not occurring or being promoted in this type of situation. We should strive to never completely tap ourselves out of our energy to act, for that is when we are no longer in a position of readiness and generosity for what comes our way. When our action potential is completely exhausted, we are literally not in a state to be "response-able" anymore. If there is one thing that all of us can do to help advance the evolution of human life, it is to prioritize our own peaceful way of living and being. This might mean not scheduling every moment of our days, not thinking too much about the past, or not worrying too much about the future. Trust in the workings of this magnificent manifestation of pure ordered energy to forge your next moment, your next thought, and your next breath. If you are at all curious to see what new levels of consciousness this human organism is capable of, realize that reaching these levels starts with prioritizing peace within yourself above all else. Peace within yourself promotes peace in your household, your neighborhood, your town, your country, and in turn the entirety of all life on Earth.

It may be tough to end relationships that are proving to be toxic to you physically, emotionally, or spiritually. These sorts of relationships can be with other individuals who influence you to do things to your body and minds that you recognize or know as toxic. If you dwell a bit, you should be able to identify at least one person you have met in your life who knowingly or unknowingly was doing this to you. However, toxic relationships can be with other things, too, such as a negative relationship with yourself and thinking over and over how you are no good, or an addiction to a substance or activity such as too much work, or even a toxic relationship with all of life on Earth, wanting to dominate and use it in overbearing and selfish ways. You will know if something is truly a toxin if it pulls you away from realizing your gift of the here and now, and prevents you from being ready, especially in a repeatable way over the course of many days. The amazing thing about our body and mind is that if we take the time and attention to listen to them deeply and sincerely, they will always guide us to health and always give us signals to what will create this peace within us. True peace is not rooted in avoidance, ignorance, numbness, or dominance, but in the practice of fully accepting what you are experiencing during every present moment of your life. However, due to the incredible biodiversity between all humans and their variation to surroundings and genetic makeup, the conditions for peace for one person might not be the exact same conditions for peace for another. For instance, one person might require less sleep or a different diet to maintain peace with themselves and others around them. We must all not become too proud in our ways if we are achieving consistent internal peace, as we are operating from a spacetime perspective that will never be experienced by anyone else. It is up to us to each discover these conditions, conditions that are constantly changing with our bodies and minds.

So perhaps a seeming paradox at first, the absolute best thing you can ever do to be selfless and care for the collective of life is to prioritize care for yourself. However, this does not mean hoarding resources or money or even carrying a selfish mindset. It means to the best of your ability encouraging for yourself a lifestyle where you care for your ability to stay in the here and now, so that you are as a cell in the immune system of humanity ready to react at all times to any task you find being asked of you. The larger organism knows what is needed next and has that wisdom balanced and worked out. Trust it.

Do not worry about what might be asked of you, if you will like it or not, or whether you are really being useful from one moment to the next. You always are: just stay ready. What unfolds in any next moment is intimately connected to billions of years of incredible evolutionary and devolutionary history and is beyond your control anyway. Whether you happen to keep awareness of it or not, your health, presence, readiness, responsibility, and peace is needed for all of humanity to flourish. I need you. We all need you. You were born for this.

Who Lives with You in Your House?

Take a moment to think about who you feel like you matter or have mattered to in this life. Parents perhaps? Siblings? Friends? At the core of it, the very word "mattered" implies that you had your physical presence of matter near to these people for a significant amount of time or in a way that created meaning to them. You may have heard someone saying that another person is "all that matters" to them, or that someone "means the world" to them. Certainly, we all have people in our lives that we feel we can relate to better than others, or those we feel have done more for us than others. We have people that we have allocated a greater portion of moments being with or tried to help. It has been discovered that for most people, they have at most about five relationships that feel very close to them, and then up to about 150 more that are of various levels of closeness, but not as close. This is about the maximum number of people we can keep meaningful relationships with at one time. Of course, there may be someone you know that you have not seen in years, but they are typically not on your mind. In theory, this number comes about due to the approximate number of humans that were part of a tribe in past years. From fossil remains, we know that up until just a few thousand years ago, humans would live and travel together in groups no larger than about 150. Our long history interacting with our environment helped decide that was a good number needed to ensure survival, and we found a stability around that number for a couple hundred thousand years. That stability had to do with available food sources, water, climate, the day's length, our average lifespan, the frequency of babies being born, and many other factors. Once in a great while, tribes might come across one another, but humans generally wanted to stay healthy and ready to help in service of this group and this group only. It was the difference between surviving and not. At the heart of it, for thousands of years the tribe was the most ordered human organism that existed. Our minds are still deeply designed and constructed to operate within this tribal framework.

We see evidence of tribal existence when we look around and see how societies are typically constructed around beliefs, activities, goods production, and providing of services. Religious worship places, schools, companies, and neighborhoods are some of the entities we may say that we belong to or are a member of. It is as if every advertisement we see is an invitation to join yet another tribe in some way. It can be easy, understandable, and convenient to look over at one of the other tribal-type entities and feel emboldened to compete for resources, just like tribes did long ago. Generally, each entity touts some perceivable competitive advantage they have over another. This type of thinking can quickly get us into believing that if we belong to certain tribes, we are superior to others in some way. Remembering the idea of holonic thinking, though, superiority in the truest sense is a temporary illusion and can damage our ability to be healthy by envisioning others as "not us." If they are not in your tribe, you could reason it is perfectly acceptable to not spend your precious life moments being present and ready to help them when you are feeling moved to do so. Even worse, during war or imprisonment conditions, completely disassociating with other groups of humans can allow us to see others as threatening obstacles to be killed or dominated.

The tribe is a convenient unit to think in and serves many useful functions for the human organism. However, the truly great victories in history are always when there is a shared peaceful collaboration between such tribes, as cities, nations, and collectives of nations emerged. Life has been doing it for billions of years, over time building toward more and more ordered levels of collaborative complexity and networks evident in all species to have ever lived. Each entity in existence is always there to serve an important function linking itself to what comes next. We cannot talk about peace between tribes if we do not have the tribes to speak of. So yes, in both my mind and yours, there is a tendency to claim our tribes and seek to defend them to help ensure both our and the tribe's survival. It is what humans have done for thousands of generations. However, if our human collective organism is to gain higher orders of consciousness, we need to recognize that the real potential of tribes occurs when they are collectives of peaceful, understanding, present individuals that are together ready to help whatever is asked and needed of them from moment to moment. When this is done in a way that negates superiority or viewing others as a perceived threat, beautiful outcomes are inevitable. Those who operate differently are committing themselves and their tribes to an unhealthy way of life. In the same way you look to your own "tribes" of cells that make up your organs to coexist peacefully within your own body, ready and willing to help one another to ensure your continued survival, so must these inter-tribal organs of humanity do the same to ensure its long-standing health.

It is an incredible achievement to be able to realize yourself as a critical member of just one super-tribe of humanity. However, remembering creatures like our LUCA, archaea, bacteria, eukaryotes, plants, sea life, and animals must also be part of the system we stay mindful of that we are also a part of. We literally owe our lives to them and must strive to see them as equals. Within all of humanity, it might be complete bliss to create a peaceful way of being for us all, but we cannot think of serving only our needs in achieving this. This is akin to a collective sort of selfishness. When we are stuck in buildings all day, in front of screens, or in highly populated cities, it can be easy to forget our connection and relationship to all of the natural life that is around us. We may rarely see forests, mountains, savannahs, rivers, and lakes in their true naturally balanced state. Our food may be so processed that we do not even take a moment to think of it as life, or a creature that once had a home and a history. Just because it may not be in front of us does not mean that it does not matter or is not important in having gotten us to our present moment. It just means *we* have forgotten. True peace within any human or any form of human tribe cannot be sustained unless moments are taken to feel and remember your connection to life, the Earth, and the universe: the balance between what your body and mind are able to do and the order you are borrowing from each and every life form that goes into your mouth; the balance between all the cities, structures and inventions we build and the natural resources required to do it; and the balance between the Earth itself and all the surrounding objects in space. You do not just belong to one family, one house, one tribe, or even one super-tribe: you belong to all of life and the universe itself. You are both the self and the collective.

Chapter 6: Life and Death

The Good and the Bad, or Just the Necessary?

Think about the last time you referred to a day you had, or even something you heard, saw, or ate, as "good" or "bad." We tend to say things like "That was really good!" or "That was so bad!" quite frequently. But what exactly is it that makes anything that way? Take for example a sweet dessert that you may enjoy and think of as good. Typically, your sensory perception of good comes from some activation of neurotransmitters in our brain such as serotonin, dopamine, oxytocin, and endorphins. While the names are less important, what is more important is that all the forms of organisms that came before us helped lead to a chemical system present in our brains and bodies that was tuned to help us survive, multiply, and form connective bonds between each other. So, what exactly makes that dessert good?

Is it that other people say it is good and that it is generally available and easy to get? Is it the sugar it contains that makes it taste good? Looking a bit deeper on sugar, it has not been refined until relatively recently in human history, and for most of our years here on Earth, sugar was relatively rare. If someone came across sugar, it was to their advantage to eat it, as it would break down easily and provide their body with a nice supply of energy to keep alive. If they found and ate a lot of it, all the better because if the body had too much, it would store it as body fat to use later. Therefore, eating lots of sugar helped ensure that you and the human species would be able to survive yet another day. Or does the dessert taste good because of the fats it contains? Consuming plant and animal fats is also advantageous for a similar reason based on survivability. So, when eating a tasty dessert, billions of years of life developed in such a way as to give us encouraging signals and help lead us to call it "good." However, we know that eating too many sweet desserts is not healthy for us. Based on available food sources and lifestyles thousands of years ago, it was extremely rare for someone to come across so much sugar and fat, as well as refrain from sharing it with the rest of their tribe. Today, this is not the case. As sugar has increased its availability around the world, the typical person now eats over forty times the amount they did about 300 years ago. We discover that this increase in sugar intake over prolonged time is responsible for all sorts of "bad" things that pull at our quality of life, such as obesity, cancer, diabetes, and erratic moods.

The same type of thinking can be applied to something other than sugar or fat, and we find time and again that a sensory "good" thing is that which activates the action of neurotransmitters, but that the same thing crosses over to "bad" when the action level due to that thing is too frequent or where the body in tandem is having to work hard to neutralize an intoxicant so it is no longer dangerous to our system. You might have heard the more common wisdom of taking everything in moderation. Once there is "too much," whatever level that is for your body's physiology, instead of that thing helping your sense of well-being, it starts to harm it. Addictions, which can take almost endless forms, are strong examples of this. With some exceptions, many chemical addictions have roots in some substance that, in a small amount as it appears in nature, your body generally accepts as good for you. Chewing a bit of a tobacco leaf, or a coca leaf, or poppy seed, or ingesting just a bit of alcohol from rotting fruit all encourage your body's functioning and well-being. Doing these things were relatively rare thousands of years ago, and it was not common to be exposed to high levels of the addictive chemicals in such plants over the course of a lifetime. However, once we learned to process, concentrate, and widely distribute the addictive compounds, it resulted in millions of people around the world getting hooked on nicotine, cocaine, heroin and its derivatives, and alcohol. Behavioral addictions follow the same type of pattern. Gambling, for instance, draws on our ability to try things in which the outcomes appear to be less certain. It was an advantage to human survival over thousands of years to be able to get excited about trying to hunt and capture a large animal, not knowing whether you will be successful in getting it. Most all plants and animals have some sense of gambling or trying things for which the outcome is distributed in a broadly statistical and unpredictable way. On and on we could go with these types of things, but however we follow it down, the "good" and "bad" seem to represent different ideas of a complete causal manifestation to us. If one person says something is "good for them," in their perception that thing, contingent on its quantity and frequency, helps them to eventually activate certain neurotransmitters and create a sense of peace and well-being along with perhaps an extension of their life, even if the feeling is extremely short-lived. If one person says something is "bad for them," this process is not happening, and that same thing could be removing layers of important order their bodies or minds have worked over much time to create.

Things get a bit trickier once we zoom out away from the individual, though. As difficult as it may be to realize what is good for you, when more people are involved, the matter complicates quickly. If you have ever tried to settle on a "best" way to do something in a large group of people, the way that is going to represent the greatest good for the collective, it will not be long until you find significant disagreement between the members if they are all voicing honest opinions. After all, since we are each a rich history of unique spacetime existences, having experienced entirely different physical and mental capabilities, it should be no surprise to find a difference in perceptions of good and bad. If we are all being honest about our perceptions with each other, it seems like it must be that way. Even very basic ideas, such as saying that having food to eat is always good, having shelter for warmth and protection is always good, and being able to travel from one place to another is always good, can be contentious. There are many who will temporarily disagree that having food to eat is good, if they are fasting for some purpose. Some may be wishing to forgo shelter for a while to find out how resilient their bodies are, and some may tout that meditating completely still and quiet will be the good thing for them while in that mode. The greater point here is that there is no one thing that exists in our current world or imagination that will ever be in an absolute sense perceived as either good or bad in everyone's experience across all times, not even this precious gift of life itself.

It is both freeing and important to realize that "good" and "bad" are most often used as short-cut words to help describe temporary passing perceptions generated by your more than 60 trillion interdependent cells interacting with the universe around you. For example, if someone around you thinks that a certain airplane is good and you do not, remembering ourselves as manifestations of infinite pure ordered energy, that is perfectly how things are supposed to be. Just keep presence and readiness around that person's viewpoint when engaging with them. Perhaps they really enjoy the ability to visit loved ones far away, or the valuable perspective they get being up in the clouds and seeing how everything down below looks so small. Perhaps you are focused on a fear of flying and think it to be unsafe, along with not liking the air pollution it

creates. Nobody must be the absolute right or wrong one --
both are equally valid reactions to the same thing. If both
people engaging fully recognize this, there is no longer a desire
to dominate their perception with yours or feel threatened
when someone thinks or acts differently than you. In fact, that
you are having differing perceptions and reactions allows you
a real opportunity to sense someone else's unique vantage
point and possibly integrate it into yours. Trust and accept
that because of your interaction, both of your perceptions will
necessarily be changed after your discussion, but the degree in
which that takes place is outside your control. Leave it up to
the universe to keep balancing all the moving pushes and pulls
as we believe it has always done. This frees up your mind and
allows you increased chances to peacefully coexist,
cooperate, and marvel in amazement at all the other human
cells you interact with. It allows you a real chance to add to
both your and their health, and in turn the health and ability of
the human collective organism. Your voice and your
perceptions matter very much, just as much as all of those
around you.

There is another issue present when thinking in absolute
terms around "good" and "bad" in your mind. Since we are
always limited to being in the present moment, not being able

to access all spacetimes at once, it is altogether not possible for us to decipher whether what we are encountering is objectively and absolutely one way or the other. For example, imagine you raise horses for a living, and one day a horse runs away. Was that good? Was that bad? Not knowing much around the situation, it could be either. Perhaps the horse has some knowledge it is sick and about to die, and if it stayed with the other horses, they would otherwise all get sick and die. So now was the situation good? What if the horse is completely healthy and leaves? Now is it bad? But let us say that the horse is healthy and runs away for one month but comes back with two other wild horses that you can now add to your stables. Now was the healthy horse running away still bad? Perhaps not. So, what happens if one of the new wild horses steps on your foot, crushing your bones and keeping you in bed and in pain for weeks. Was that bad? Was that good? But what if while you are recovering in bed, it causes you to reflect on your life and after you heal you decide to start a new business that you feel is much more successful and gives you much greater life satisfaction than you had before. It allows you to live a more healthy and ready life. Now was your foot getting crushed bad? All this confusion with trying to judge what is happening and has happened to you can be significant, but the confusion is exacerbated when other people are added into the mix. The two wild horses that found their way to you may otherwise have gone to a different stable if they had not found your horse that ran away. So if them coming your way was good, was it then bad for the other stable that did not receive them? It seems, perhaps, there is no way to at once properly judge the absolute merit of anything that you experience. You cannot possibly realize all the billions of years of moments leading up to what happened, the totality of what had to occur for the present moment to manifest, as well as the billions of future years that an event will affect in some way. This is why the practice of non-judgement is so important. Every time you profess to know absolutely that something or some experience is "good" or "bad" for you, just recognize that your opinion is coming from a vantage point that is completely valid, yet limited in its judgement in the greatest of degrees. Asking why bad things happen to good people is a grand question rife with judgement built into its very wording. Trust that the physical universe, manifested from infinite ordered energy, does not make errors and is giving you and everything else exactly what is needed and intended each and every moment.

If you are coming across this sort of thinking for the first time, you might be saying to yourself: *This makes absolutely no sense...of course there are good and bad things! What about murder and nuclear war and disease and people losing their jobs and tyrannies and other atrocities? Those are bad! And of course, being kind, generous, loving, and empathic are good!* However, one must be careful with making those types of absolute judgments if extremely long timescales are being considered. We collectively observe things that appear to coexist with those operating from a peaceful way of being and things that appear to influence peace on other life forms, and it is tempting to put those into a column we can most definitely label "absolutely good." After all, humans as a collective are constructed in a way that motivates and encourages connection with each other to realize ever higher levels of collective consciousness and peace. But just as all species have experienced long periods of time evolving to higher systems of order, nature deems it necessary to build in a devolving process of increasing chaos to keep balance. Remember that we are here after five major mass extinctions of life and we are a part of the less than one percent in existence today. Consider all the moments of *homo sapiens*, modern humans, history only -- forget even every life form that came before us for a bit -- and what had to unfold for you to be here in this present moment where you are at. Thousands of generations of humans had to come together in extremely specific ways and do exactly as they did for you to have been born. They had to forage, build shelter, hunt, cooperate and fight along the way. They had to collectively do a lot of things that we might call virtuous or good in order to survive. However, if five hundred generations ago a particular man did not force himself on a woman and have sex with her on a certain day, then today you are not here. If three hundred generations ago several people were not murdered in their sleep and driven from their homeland, then today you are not here. If one hundred generations ago, many people did not die of a great disease, then today you are also not here.

Here is perhaps the most important point to this -- if you are to live your life in such a way that you are able to freely marvel deeply at your gift of the incredible, unimaginable odds being born as the human form you are, if you are able to appreciate the care that the universe has taken to balance each and every push and pull in its history, if you are able to contemplate the incredible degree of dark energy existing in our universe, if you are able to grasp the unfathomable evolution of life necessary to create you, if you are able to stay present with each moment, ready to act with keen intuition, if you are able to recognize everything as one manifestation of ordered infinite energy, you must come to one eventual conclusion. The conclusion is that each and every event that has ever occurred is necessary for reasons beyond our full comprehension, and we should love, embrace, and recognize the beauty of the sum total of it as fully and completely as we are able. There only remains the love and consciousness expressed through your being, but the words "good" or "bad" are also not fitting here. We can only say that expressing this love as a way of being leads most people to a greater feeling of ever deeper connectedness, freedom, and completeness.

So, are things like rape, murder, theft, betrayal and disease objectively "bad" then, across billions and trillions of years' worth of time? It appears this cannot be so. In a relatively limited human spacetime perception, they are most always experienced as bad, and certainly cause much pain, suffering, and trauma to those connected to such experiences, but we must accept even ugly things such as these as being necessary and put into motion long ago. Often, those who have managed to make peace with those who have wronged them, their friends, or their families in the worst ways discover opportunities for deep degrees of self-love and feelings of emotional freedom through forgiveness. If we are to completely love and accept ourselves and others, then we must be ready to embrace and find love for every single event and entity that we become conscious of. Just as we cannot know true joy without true sadness, we should love and appreciate the existence of both as necessary for our current condition. Doing otherwise keeps us in a state that is of a different order of health, closes up our hearts, and sets limits on the ways we can serve as a healthy cell in the human organism.

It's A Matter of Life and Death

Up until now, we have only talked about "good" and "bad" things from the human viewpoint. Amongst humans, there is general agreement that things thought to accelerate our realization of equality, connection, physical and mental health, and education are all good things. Advancements in these sorts of things are frequently promoted, celebrated and recognized. We might imagine an ideal state where we feel like equally connected gods who have access to anyone and anything that we desire, communicating perfectly, versed in the total of all knowledge and experience, with our bodies staying perfectly healthy for an eternal length of time. While this would most likely increase the health and order of consciousness for the collective augmented human organism and unlock many new potentials unimaginable right now, it begs the question of what forms of order we would end up borrowing from to achieve this and how long nature will allow this order to continue existing. We can never forget that we are interdependent on all other life forms, both small and large from our perspective. To achieve our current state of existence, we have caged and slaughtered billions of animals, taking away their ability to socially connect and achieve the peace they may have had otherwise if allowed to roam free. We have taken billions of fish from oceans and lakes and cleared prairies and forests to build structures, grow crops, and raise cattle. Our collective activity has polluted the air, water, and earth with many materials toxic to most all life forms. Human activity has been responsible for getting rid of much biodiversity that has been in balance for millions of years. Our human organism has evolved quite quickly compared to the age of our universe and it has come at the cost of reordering and extinguishing so much of the network for all of life. If we could ask every animal and plant species, how many would say that the totality of all our accomplishments is good in their limited perspectives? Or maybe at some level they have all recognized and accepted the deeper necessary element to all of it.

We should be mindful that the order each human and every other animal needs to borrow to stay alive necessarily causes death to other entities and organisms. New life, or sustained forms of order, can only emerge from death, or the increase in chaos for another system: this is the only way nature allows it. Whether it is death to the order of the sun, death to bacterial, plant or animal life, or death to one of our skin cells about once every three seconds, death is a necessary manifestation of what we have found to be fundamentally true about the progression of order and chaos through time. Death is and always has been sacrificial throughout nature, as it has allowed all of life to evolve. It is important to not turn a blind eye to this, pretending that death is unrelated to the foods that nourish our bodies or unrelated to the homes of creatures we destroy every time we build a new house. Whether we hold it in our consciousness or not, both endless new life and endless death are processes continuously unfolding around us. Built into our desires and anticipations is a whole lot of death. Remember your favorite dessert? A lot of death is built into the creation of just one serving of it. This is something that we can spend time feeling guilt around or trying to block from our minds because it makes us feel uncomfortable. We may only want to focus on the life-giving aspect of it. However, along with everything else that is in existence, to optimize our state of health we must contemplate, accept, and embrace these forms of consequential death. Our collective human organism, to evolve its consciousness, must realize that much death must occur for us to take our next steps. The present moment is always dying for the life of the new moment to come into existence. Things that we might see as permanent must always die given enough time. The largest of institutions, the most magnificent of cities, and even the tallest of mountains must all eventually die to give way to what is realized after it. Anything you might feel attached to is destined to die in its current form, so recognizing this might allow you more peace around those attachments. Death, in this regard, can be appreciated and even celebrated for providing us our precious gift of being able to stay healthy and ready in the present moment. It does not have to be something that we shy away from talking about, or even something that we lament.

It is quite common to believe human life is more important than other life forms that have existed in the past or are present today. We appear to be created in a way that we can connect and relate more easily to things we see a reflection of ourselves in, and we typically hold a higher value around those things. In our brains, along with the brains of other primates and birds, there exist entities known as "mirror neurons" that activate either when we are doing an activity or witnessing another entity performing a similar activity. In short, it means that humans more easily connect with humans and other creatures when they see behavior that resembles their own expressions or capabilities. Think about how influential to your being it is to be with a group of happy people or a group of sad people. It feels difficult and almost impossible to both completely be present and ready to act with them and to not be happy or sad along with them. We most closely hold the lives of other humans as important partly because connecting with them is what our brains are built to do. However, at least to creatures such as birds and monkeys, they are wired to see themselves as more important compared to us. The presence of these so-called "mirror neurons" built into our biology help cause us to create hierarchies of value based on people and creatures that essentially mimic us. We might value human life above all, then perhaps other primates, and then other creatures who share a somewhat similar level of brain development or ability to express emotions we can relate to. It might be endlessly debated whether it is most important to save the whales, save the stray dogs, or save the pineapple field. In each case, we are attempting to place a value on the death of one entity on the creation of new life for another entity. After all, every time an animal dies and decays, it is providing new life for the bacteria responsible for doing so. But, just because our own experience of conscious life is more fully removed from bacteria compared to a cat, for instance, how can we accurately and objectively judge whether the cat's life is more important than the collective life of the bacteria thriving at the cost of it perishing? How can we possibly ever equate the true value of one organism's life on another? Is the life of one giraffe worth at least that of three goats? Or are the lives of one hundred tulips worth the life of one hundred thousand blades of grass? In our current societies, we are constantly making these valuations, often using money, emotions, or laws as a medium to express them, but we should realize what these valuations stem from and not get too attached to thinking of this as an ultimate form of truth but an expression of collective current belief.

Returning to the idea of holonic thinking, we must eventually concede and recognize that although our lives and other human lives may appear to be of ultimate importance from the vantage point of our consciousness and egos, we need to trust that nature has always built in the element of equity between all life forms and forms of order. Our web of life is consistently making the trade of certain life forms with others, in complex and perfectly balanced ways. It will never be up to us to decide how trades between life forms occur at all levels; rather, it is something we must accept and submit to. If your conscious human life is to end with the event of being consumed by cancer to help sustain the life of the cancerous cells inside of you, then that is the equality of your human body and its death with their life in the moments that follow. If your conscious human life ends from natural causes, resulting in a burial or cremation, the conclusion of your journey of being ordered in the way you were results in the trade of your physical human body for the life of trillions of bacteria that will consume your body over time, or the brief life of a fire as your body turns to ash. We should not believe we know some sort of static equation between any life forms, including our own. It can never be that simple. There are limitless ways to conceptualize how different life forms are created, traded, and ended. It is absolutely amazing to think of all life and death above all clinging to the assurance of balancing the moving pushes and pulls in ever creative and varied ways, always increasing the overall disorder of the universe. The totality of all life and all death is all part of the one infinite ordered energy at the base of everything. Full acceptance for all moments of your own life is also full acceptance of your own death.

What Do You Do in Your Free Time?

Much has been written, discussed, and debated around the topic of freedom, and it means different things to different people. We might say that life itself is freedom, or some might say that you become free only upon death. Some talk about freedom in the context of choice: to be able to choose what you pick off a menu or who you keep as a friend, for instance. You could say that you are free to read this book right now or free to sit or stand. Many say that freedom and free will are in the realm of human capability only and that our species is the only one able to make choices with an element of conscious intention and good or ill will. Free will can also get a bit fuzzy within humans, with many believing that you do not have free will as an infant, but that it comes at some point later in life. Certainly, there is a lot of variety in the way we view ourselves as either free or not in the context of the entire universe.

So, what is it precisely that gives us this free will and sets us apart from the rest of the animal kingdom? Is it our superior physical abilities? The capabilities for all five of our senses are easily surpassed by other animals who can smell, taste, see, hear, and feel with much greater capacities than us. There are many animals that can run faster, jump higher, react quicker, and have much better protective armor compared to our skin. Not to mention most all of them have been in existence for magnitudes of time longer than we have. Is it our capacity for emotion that sets us apart? Perhaps our emotions are comprised of more layers than other animals, but we have found evidence for all major basic human emotions reflected in primates and other animals. They have emotional landscapes that include empathy, jealousy, greed, apathy, sadness, joy, and happiness. Elephants are known to spend days grieving next to close relatives for days on end due to their emotional states. Is it our capacity for language? It is miraculous to me that I am able to communicate ideas to you in this type of medium, and as far as we know other animals cannot write to each other. However, the transference of information between other animals certainly takes place in other forms, often very different than how we do it. Most all animal species "talk" to each other in some way, whether it be through vibrations sent through the ground, sounds and calls in the air, scents they produce to express approval or disapproval, or colors they turn to get attention from each other. Is it our ability to work in teams? We see groups of animals working together to hunt all the time, sacrificing for one another, and using similar battle formations and tactics against their prey that we have used in times of war. This type of behavior also shows they can anticipate and think ahead, strategizing and optimizing their actions. So, what element that is distinctly human would give us a freedom or free will not found in the rest of the animal kingdom?

Consequently, it may be that we are able to conceive of such a thing. We frequently celebrate and find pride in our race because of our imagination and our capacity to consider questions that appear much too abstract for any other species. While monkeys may have two hundred or more distinct sounds to convey meaning for describing the details around what they see, the English language alone has more than 400,000 distinct words. These are all necessary to reflect the layers of complexity found within our brains and the desire to express these layers of perceived complexity and order with so many words. And sure, other animals can plan a hunt, but can they create a plan to realize something as complicated as a company with 500,000 employees, compose a symphony, or build a space station that orbits the Earth? Our plans can span over much greater timelines, with a greater degree of pattern recognitions, and greater coordination between massive collectives of humans all over the Earth. It is certainly something to behold. Within many domains, humans are currently able to conceptualize and realize more complex forms of order whose parallels cannot be found anywhere else in the universe. It may be tempting to think that recognizing certain effects that follow cause in a variety of domains gives us freedom, and that we are free to build and say what we want, but it still seems we are not "free" in the sense that many people believe.

Let us return for a moment to some of the basic truths that we have discovered as a species so far. The word "discovered" literally means that we un-covered something that already existed, that we exposed it. Science has brought us much "discovery," but there is no freedom on our end in what is under those covers. Science, as a process, illuminates the idea that we must first observe something that is already occurring in nature to realize some pattern in how it operates. There is no physical freedom for us in deciding whether we would like a chemical reaction to occur or how tall a plant will grow under given conditions. We do not decide the effects that follow cause; we only witness them. In the scientific process, what "is" is the element of value, not what we hope or wish is there for whatever reason we might have. The "is" of what has been discovered so far regarding the nature of the universe around us has been touched on in some of the previous chapters. Some of these things might cause us discomfort, but when we approach things from many different angles, independent of bias, across all areas of the world, and keep perceiving the same thing, there is an untenable element of deeper truth potential in that. Whether we like it or not, if we want to align with what is and feel truly free, we must accept that we will never know exactly where or when we are in relation to the totality of spacetime itself and acknowledge its relative nature. We must accept that we are both one and many distinct life forms simultaneously. We must accept that all life forms have vastly detailed deep histories and ways of interacting, having formed their atoms from stars and ultimately stemming from infinite pure energy. We must accept that all mass and objects we see around us are fundamentally all balanced and moving pushes and pulls. We must accept that what is happening to the total order of the universe tells us that everything we see can never be permanent across all times to come. These are realizations we have come to through a process unfolding for billions of years, not choices of how we might want the universe to behave.

Perhaps a suitable analogy about a true free will in the physical realm, or our ability to control the cause before the effect, can be made if we consider a movie that has been recorded in a digital format. It is shown in rich color on a large theatre screen with life-like surround sound. You experience the movie as the opening scene plays. You perceive a sight and a sound that seem just like real life, but what are you "actually" seeing and hearing? You are seeing a series of still frames that refresh fast enough so you cannot notice just one alone. The frames must appear in just the right order at a specific time. In each frame, you are seeing a large grid of pixels, or small areas that have both a distinct color and brightness. The color and brightness information for each pixel is displayed according to some sort of a reference table that the projection system has on a computer. The reference table has codes that say something to the effect of "For the pixel located here, if the first number I give you is 435, then display this green color. If the second number I give you is 1333, then make it this bright." The information for the pixel, before that, is stored somewhere in a physical state that has patterns corresponding to these numbers, on something with tiny magnets for instance. It is therefore difficult for our minds to make the leap to say, "what I'm actually looking at is the result of a bunch of small magnets creating a chain reaction that sends specific signals to my eye that are together making me perceive colorful motion." In a similar way, the sounds reaching your ear are also stored in slices and are generated much the same way. Anything in digital format can thus be reduced to patterns of digits, but we do not experience digits: we experience something much more magnificent and layered. But materials that can store and transmit things by "digits" is the singular idea of how the movie ultimately is able to manifest, much like the fundamental collections of moving pushes and pulls allow our experience to manifest.

Now let us think about the experience as you watch the movie. You sit as each frame unfolds before you, just as the producers and directors have designed them to be. If it is a suspenseful movie, you might be on the edge of your seat, pleading with the characters to do certain things or not, with your mirror neurons greatly activated. If it is a mystery movie, you might think you know exactly what is going on and that you have it all figured out. You might feel like you have some sense of control or knowledge in that experience, and even brag a bit to someone sitting near you saying "Watch: I know exactly what is going to happen!" only to find that there is a clever plot twist at the end that escaped you. You watch the movie, frame by frame in anticipation, and it is a new experience for you. But, before the movie started, all those frames were already decided and defined. From your viewpoint, the characters might be able to make certain choices in real time, but this is just an illusion. The last frame of the movie was already in place, the digits making up the movie already in an uncompromised state. You might be happy after the movie or disappointed, but these may just be the result of the degree of match between how you wanted the experience to be and what it was.

What nature has revealed to us is that the history of the universe can be thought of like one gigantic movie cut into an extremely large number of successive frames whose order represents the arrow of time. Each frame, containing the sum of all moving pushes and pulls, is intimately connected to the ones both immediately before and after it by fundamental rules and laws about what will and will not happen. There is no element of freedom here so to speak because the rules and laws of nature dictate the condition of "must" and a distinct determination. Many phenomena we model as random distributions still fall into this - there will be a specific distribution of outcomes that will converge and smooth out over time, so this too illuminates another type of "must." We are not able to predict how the next frame unfolds with perfect knowledge, but the totality of our universe knows precisely what needs to come next. Each universal movie frame is both unique to the others and stitched in novel ways to the frames before and after it, keeping an ultimate balance through several underlying mechanisms that usually escape our awareness. Since we are inside of this universe, we cannot choose whether to be part of this fabric or not. It is as if we are characters inside this grand movie, with the perception that we can do as we wish, but ultimately the director that has set the universe in motion has already created, determined, and watched everything in it, from the first to the last frame from all vantage points. What we believe to be free choices we ascribe to our doing and will only is purely an illusion for the observing director and the fabric of the universe itself. This movie can always unfold and progress in one way only. But to us, we sit as a small pixel existing for just a few visual frames or for the briefest snippet of sound. Thinking like this might cause fear, denial, or sadness if we focus on just one pixel or snippet. It can make us feel very anxious and lost. But if we focus on the whole movie, remembering the attention to detail and all the beauty it represents, we may become peaceful, feeling more connected, ready, responsible, and alive. Through this process, we reach our truest experience of creativity and freedom.

Are You Out of Your Mind?

There is something else noteworthy when considering whether we really have free will to carry out an action. We might think of free will as being something beyond our physical bodies, something nebulous inside of us, or that which arises as a consequence of the coordinated workings of all our cells and spirit. Alternately, we might see it as something we possess that allows us control of causes before an effect. Whenever we mention cause and effect though, we need to connect back to the idea of spacetime and a direction for it. In our perception, we would say that something was first initiated by a cause, and the effect followed. You might say "I took a step forward and then I moved" and perceive that first the step happened, and then your movement followed. However, that is not altogether accurate, as the movement forward was initiated the moment your foot first pushed against the ground or floor. There was a delay in your awareness, and so by the time your body and mind were able to perceive and notice what was happening, the cause has already influenced the effect. Delays of perceiving "present time" like this are built into every organism and into the nature of spacetime itself. Remember that the speed of light is the fastest speed that anything can go and is also the speed of cause and effect in tandem with interacting forces that cause effects. Therefore, when dealing with any entity a distance away from you, there is a lag with what we might refer to as the present moment, or "now."

Some of the furthest objects we have observed in space represent the greatest time delays. The most distant galaxies we can detect are over 13 billion light-years away. That means that the light we are seeing from that galaxy began its journey that amount of time ago. More than 13 billion years later, traveling at the universal speed limit, it has finally reached us. What we are seeing is not "actually" there right now; it was there a long time ago, before the creation of the Earth and life. The cause was initiated billions of years ago, but just now we receive the corresponding effect. Every object we see in the sky is always an observation of what that object was, not what it currently is. The further it is out, the more pronounced this effect. Many stars we see are several hundred light-years away. The North Star is over 300 light-years away, so if you see it in the sky, you are observing it as it was perhaps six or more generations of humans ago. The closest non-sun star to us, Proxima Centauri, is just over 4 light-years away, so that is as young as the star light gets. When you see the sun setting on the horizon "right now," you are seeing where it was about 8 minutes ago. Our closest celestial neighbor, the moon, comes in with just over a second of delay.

When we bring this realization closer to things right in front of us, our minds do a wonderful job of stitching everything that we are really seeing in the past to create what feels like a singular "now" moment. There are other limits that increase our perceptual delay with the actual "now" other than the speed of light, however. The light rays we perceive must first enter our eyes, be converted to an electrical signal at our optic nerve, then sent to our brain for processing and realizing. To the best of your body's ability, what you believe to be "now" actually occurred about 0.08 seconds ago. By the time our brains receive a signal, process it, and react to it as quickly as possible, for the average human that time is about 0.15 seconds. If there is conscious thought involved, the time goes up significantly. And compared to some other species, this time is incredibly slow. Some fish can react to signals they receive in as little as 0.005 seconds! Let us reimagine all the individual movie frames that comprise the universe and the totality of its history. To truly have free will to influence effect from a decided, self-generated cause, we need to compensate for this delay. It is as if 100 frames would first be played, and then we go back 100 frames earlier, decide to change something with our free will decision, and then have the 100 frames play again in exactly the same way by orienting all of the universe's balanced pushes and pulls to how they were. But if we really did change something, the frames cannot unfold in the same way. We would be going backward in time and changing the actual nature of the past, which inasmuch we know is not possible and would require an infinite amount of energy we are not known to possess. In real time, the cause and the effect action are always occurring at light speed and no slower, so anything below the speed of light, including anything that possesses mass, is not in synchronization with the initiation of cause and effect. Though, it does not completely rule out the possibility for true free will if we consider things in realms we currently do not understand.

You might be thinking to yourself "but if we do not really have any free will, then things like morality and the meaning of life go away!" This does not need to be true. We are just not physically "free" outside the constraints that nature has put on us. We are not free to have effect precede cause as we define it with time as our reference. This does not mean we cannot feel like we have free will or even celebrate this concept, but it does mean that the essence that is the pure ordered infinite energy is that which is truly guiding the next moments of our lives, and will always have a level of awareness that we may strive for, but will not be able to ever reach while in our human form. It does not have to remove any idea of morality or life meaning. In fact, it may enhance both and help us drift away from a self-centered or selfish way of being, informing us that something beyond our being is in complete control.

Another thing which may be a useful realization is that any conscious or even subconscious thought arising in our mind always arises after an emotional feeling or physical sensation. For example, first the nerves in our skin transmit the signal to our brains corresponding to either pleasure or pain, and after a short delay the thought originates around a judgement about whether it feels good or bad. If we are scared by something or sense danger, we first recoil back or our heart rate increases before we can think about the fact that we are scared. It is only then that we match up the two. If something funny happens while we are completely present, first the laugh comes and then we think about how or why it is funny to us. Our raw emotions and sensory input are all time-delayed reactions to our physical environment, but they are much closer to the actual present moment than our thoughts are. If we are striving to be aligned with the true present moment of what is and be with it, we need to accept that we need to literally follow our hearts as closely and quickly as possible. The further the time delay between when our hearts are and when our minds accept our hearts, the greater the level of confusion for us internally. As the time gap between the two gets larger, it becomes increasingly difficult to realize a feeling of peace and alignment with what is and about what controls us. The result is that our health becomes compromised as we are not as able to act as a cell ready to help the larger human and life organism. Things like depression and regret can arise when the thoughts in our mind are focused on where our hearts were a significant amount of time ago, so that we are constantly revisiting past states of being, either perceived to be good or bad. Things like anxiety and fear can arise when the thoughts in our mind are focused on where we believe our hearts will be a significant amount of time into the future. As those future moments unfold, there may be a mismatch between the imagined state of your heart and where it ends up. To add a further complication to both depression and anxiety, while you are stuck in either of those tracks, you are missing out on the beauty and mystery around your present moment that is about to be gone forever. A significant amount of these moments can make any life feel more closely like a death. If you find yourself in either of these situations, the best solution is always to literally "go out of your mind" in a way that encourages it to reconnect with your present heart and helps you regain focus on the incredible reality before you.

How Old Are You?

One of the most fascinating things about life is the particular way in which each life develops. In humans and in so many other species, the expression of sex is tantamount to continuing the next generation of humans by replacing aging cells in the human organism. We are built for sexual expression, though there is a stark difference between human males and females in the amount of reproductive material they can produce in their lifetime. A female is born with most all the eggs she will ever have, about one million, and is able to create a few more after she is born. However, during her years of fertility, her body will release only 300 to 400 of them at a frequency similar to the moon cycles. A male, by contrast, can produce around 1500 sperm every second! So, about five times the number of sperm for a male in a single second compared to the number of eggs the female will release in an entire lifetime. Playing with the odds of you being born with the genetic material you have illuminates one more layer of infinite complexity. Assuming traditional methods of pregnancy, not only did your parents, and parents of your parents, et cetera, have to find each other first and have sex with each other while the conditions inside the female were just right, but the possible combinations of what may have arisen is staggering. Over the course of their lifetime, males can produce over 500 billion sperm, and as many sperm as there are people on Earth once every few months. Having just one of these make contact with a female's egg is remarkable. Each egg produced is only alive for about 24 hours, and the sperm must propel themselves forward a distance of at least 1,000 times their own length to reach it. They move toward the ·egg in a spiral motion using their available energy to spin a perfectly efficient flagellar motor that causes their tail to whip back and forth during the journey. However, this is just the beginning of a new human life.

After a sperm and egg meet, provided the female has the right conditions present in her uterus, they immediately know what to do with each other. There is awareness at some level that they are to work together and begin fusing with one another to create a new physical and spiritual being. The phases of development that occur after this inside a woman's body over the next nine months or so are so magnificent, as they parallel all the features of billions of years of species evolution in a highly compacted time frame. The sperm and egg, at first solitary creatures, begin creating a colony of independent human cells by the power of their union. The healthy cells remain ready to transform and have awareness of where they need to station themselves to lay the groundwork for a backbone, an eye, a heart, or a brain. As we begin our human lives, we are like our LUCA, surrounded by water in relative warm darkness and safety, cells multiplying, moving in colonies, and striving to create something with consciousness greater than themselves. As the human embryo develops, other curious features are present that remind us of our evolution and oneness with other life forms. Just like in the embryos of birds, fish, and reptiles, we see in the human embryo a glimpse of a not-yet-completely-formed common ancestor that has a brain, eyes, spine, gills, nubs on the side of the gills, and a tail. Eventually our tail will retract into our body, the nubs will become arms and legs, and our gills will transform to lungs to breathe air, but at this early stage we appear more like a bird or fish than not. Instead of occurring more slowly over billions and millions of years, we instead start differentiating in appearance from the other life forms in just a matter of days.

After about two months' time, that single sperm and egg have managed to multiply and coordinate that multiplication in a way that the growing human has the beginnings of all the organs it will ever need in its lifetime, including the brain, heart, kidneys, liver and intestines. There is not yet the ability for human conscious thought as we might know it, but it is interesting to imagine what the experience of consciousness was when you were just two months in the womb. All the while, your growing body being built for your human life is already undergoing much death, passing dead cells and other waste through the amniotic fluid and umbilical cord to the mother. This cord was also passing to your body oxygen-rich blood and other nutrients from the mother to give the baby the order it needs to grow and develop. Over the course of a few months, beyond any of your control, two fusing entities that started the chain of events transformed into a creature capable of breathing air, digesting food, hearing, seeing, sensing touch, regulating heartbeat, and so much more. At the time of your birth, you had about 100 billion brain cells, with the neurons interconnected in such a way that your brain could sustain brain waves allowing you to realize ever-evolving layers of consciousness.

If this is not fantastic enough, the volume of that initial sperm and egg you started from becomes multiplied by around 100 billion once you are fully grown. Something that contained all the instructions to build you began as the size of the period at the end of this sentence. This is commensurate with taking a group of 100 adults and having their volume become that of the entirety of Mount Everest. Multiplying your volume by 100 billion is more of a jump in size than if you were suddenly able to transform to the size of all human beings on Earth alive right now. Yet, we know this awesome jump in size has already occurred for every person on Earth who is fully grown. The intelligence necessary to carefully construct you precisely in your current form has been at work for quite some time, and has taken a lot of care to do so.

What Do You Think About That?

Brains are perhaps the most fascinating organs that we possess and can study. Numerous volumes have been written in elaborate detail about the workings of the brain, the names for each part, and what each is responsible for. The building blocks used for cross-connection and transmitting electrical signals in all brains are made of neurons. Neurons, in some creatures such as jellyfish, are not used to help regulate the body, but rather to help push them along in water. So in nature they are used for more than one function. The bodies of fruit flies and ants possess on the order of 100,000 of these neurons, an octopus about 100 million, or 1000 times more by comparison, and giraffes, primates, and humans more than 10 billion. The only animal found to have more neurons in their body than a human is the African elephant with over 100 billion neurons. A body and brain's level of functionality does not just depend on the number of neurons, but also on the number of synapses, or connections between neurons. These interconnections are key to what make brains so varied in their functionality. Each neuron in the human brain is thought to be connected to about 7,000 other neurons, so that the brain's true power arises from this hyper-connectivity much more than the neurons themselves. Creating and maintaining this level of complex order comes at a relatively high cost to us, with our brains constituting only about 1 percent of our total body mass but 20 percent of our energy intake.

It may be tempting to think of our brain as one single entity, but its construction is sectioned off in many intricate ways. One of the more fascinating realizations of the human brain is that closest to the base of it are parts commonly found developed in creatures who evolved before us. There are different glands that help regulate our sleep, hormone secretions, and bone and muscle growth. Also, at the base of the brain are parts called "lobes" responsible for things such as pain sensation, memory, and emotion. As we get a bit further from the base of the brain, lobes are responsible for things like sensory input, temperature sensation, and spatial perception. It is not until we get the furthest from the brain stem that we reach the frontal lobe, which is essentially right behind our foreheads. Our frontal lobes are much more developed and interconnected than in any other species, and they are responsible for our ability to judge, plan, problem-solve, concentrate, and interpret the meaning of the characters you are reading in this sentence. They are also responsible for our concept of self and self-awareness. This is a crucial feature that enables our capacity for abstract thought and reasoning and gives you that "voice" inside your head you might have as you read these words. However, the frontal lobe is the last physical stop for sensory input in our entire brain, so when some form of stimulation occurs, this is another way to see how our heart naturally comes before our head. Our true emotional and physical reactions to something are already formed well before we can filter, reason, judge, and become aware of them in our frontal lobe as they are processed. These are things such as fear, aggression, embarrassment, hunger, and sexual urges. It is only when we attempt to separate the "what is" and "what we want to be" that extra energy needs to be allocated to our synapses, which carries the possibility of leaving us mentally exhausted if this happens too often.

Our consciousness and awareness then are not completely different than that of other life forms, but it does carry a different quality due to the way our brain is constructed. Our bodies have many forms of awareness that coexist at various levels below our thinking brains, which we often term as "subconscious." We might think of much of our subconscious as a real way to be in connection to the experience of several other animal life forms who experience emotion, pain, and exhaustion. It is as if packed into us is a modified version of all of them plus a bit of us. However, an intriguing feature unique to the human brain is that when we are born, our frontal lobe is significantly underdeveloped. The ability for us to realize our sense of self or reason anything out is not yet there. The first time it really picks up its development is between 6 and 12 months of age. Our frontal lobe is one of the last parts of our body to fully develop, occurring around the age of 25 or so. So, while it is being utilized our entire lives, the quality and ability for different types of conscious awareness are biologically not possible until it is fully developed. By design, we were built such that we require a necessary period before our full conscious capacity is unlocked. If you happen to be under the age of around 25, it is exciting to realize that there is more brain development to come in this arena, where you will more readily be able to make connections between abstract thoughts and ideas.

A useful metric that has been used to help make sense of our quality of consciousness is that of brain wave frequency. In general, when your brain wave frequency is highest, you feel a heightened sense of awareness and readiness with your outside world. When your brain wave frequency is lowest, you are most detached from awareness of that world. For ease of thinking around this topic, let us define some of the brain wave frequency bands and what they are responsible for.

Delta waves, from about 0.5 to 3 electrical cycles per second, are associated with healing, empathy, and deep dreamless sleep. Theta waves, from about 3 to 8 cycles per second, are associated with vivid imagery, intuition, deep meditation, and our fears. These are the waves in our brain when we feel like we are just about asleep. Alpha waves, from about 8 to 12 cycles per second, are when we are in a restful, alert, calm and consciously aware state. These waves are associated with learning and allow us to integrate at once what the mind and body are doing. Beta waves occur from about 12 to 38 cycles per second and are associated with a good portion of our waking moments, helping us problem-solve, reason, and make judgements. Gamma waves are anything above 38 cycles per second and are the brain waves with the highest frequency. They are the most subtle to detect and have been found to be highly active when people are in states of feeling connection to others and the universe. Gamma waves are associated with consciousness expansion, a shift in personal perception, and a deep sense of spirituality.

Just like the cells in our bodies work together in harmony to form our organs, and our organs work together to keep us alive, and the parts of our brain work together to create the totality of our human awareness, so are all of these brain waves needed for us to completely realize ourselves. Together, the right distribution of these brain waves help develop a version of us that is able to be healthy and in a state of readiness to connect with the moment and whatever and whoever comes our way. Perhaps not surprisingly, the alpha waves associated with this way of being are balanced right in the middle, but we need moments where the brain is running on other frequencies in order to promote the quality of the moments we exist in the alpha state. We need deep, restful sleep, but we also need moments to help reason and solve problems unfolding before us, and we need some moments where we realize and sense a shift in our state of being. As beta waves are above the energy needed for alpha, if we spend too much time in this area, constantly thinking and reasoning all our waking hours, we will fatigue and become less efficient and off-balance. Too many delta and theta waves and we will feel sluggish and unmotivated. Gamma waves by comparison are a bit more fleeting for most people and less is known about them. They are above the rates at which neurons in the brain can activate, so it is possible they may be drawing their energy from an altogether different region of the body, its surroundings, or from another source. Some people who have practiced focused ways of being and meditation for several years have been found to have a much higher prominence of gamma waves in their brains. It is as if everything always feels open and connected for them, and they are in a constant state of preparedness and synchronicity for whatever happens.

Although reaching a condition where every human on Earth is living each day with continual gamma waves running through their brains might be thought of as a sort of utopia, we know there is a necessary progression and evolution toward being in that state. Think about the earliest memory that you have. How old were you? Five or older? Four perhaps? Three maybe? Two years old? The day you were born was pretty special and life-changing, so why can we not remember that? It can be a bit unsettling to realize that you were born and alive in this world for a period of time you have absolutely no memory of. Although very much biologically alive, the early creature the sperm and egg came together to create was for a long time what we might think of as being consciously asleep. Living, but in a much different state of awareness. It turns out children from the age of newborn to about two years old have brain activity that corresponds to delta waves only. This means that for the first two years of life, you were only a receiver and reactor to the events that unfold around you, in tune with an internal landscape, similar to an adult that is in deep sleep. In fact, you could go from waking to deep sleep in a matter of seconds. In this mode, you were not able yet to reason or think in the way you can now or form coherent memories. Your brain accepted stimulation however it entered you and then imprinted on your brain. If you saw a behavior around you, you simply tried to mirror and mimic it without reasoning it out. Kids around this age are also highly emotionally sensitive and empathic, frequently smiling when others around them smile, and getting upset when others around them are upset. Emotions you sensed from others around you during these ages formed your early impressions of emotional normalcy.

Between about the ages of two and six years old, your brain was only capable of cycling between delta and theta waves. Around these ages, you were very connected to imagination, daydreaming, and an internal world. You were still not able to reason things out in predictive and rational ways. Whatever someone told you, you probably accepted it as true without much questioning. If someone told you they were a dinosaur, you were able to really see them as a dinosaur. If someone told you that you could jump from the Earth and land on the moon, you might say, "Okay, let's do it!" If you were imagining something and an adult told you it was not in fact real, you likely got a bit angry because it was not in synchronization with your viewpoint and perceived truth at that time. When adults are hypnotized, they are typically in this state, as well as several animals in their wakeful state. Somewhere between around five and eight years old, your brain started to transition more and more time devoted to being in the alpha state. You could say that this was the first opportunity you had to start really becoming conscious of the external world and its workings, while still being heavily influenced by your imagination and internal world. In this state, learning new information is very effective, and so learning new skills at these ages was relatively easy for you. Starting around eight years of age, you started expanding your brain waves into the beta frequencies and gained the capacity for reasoning, recognizing more patterns on your own, and for abstract thought. It is often said that around seven or eight years old, a child reaches "the age of reason," and this is what is going on in their brains at that time. After this time, as your brain continued to grow and develop, it kept gaining capacity to think and evaluate the external world around it in new and varied ways. Again, if you are under 25, it is likely that this process is silently continuing right now inside of your brain, adding the capacity for higher and higher beta frequencies.

However, if we are giving our brain enough things that are toxic to it, this growth may stop early and never continue.

When we pause to think about the concept of us having "one life," in some sense it may be useful to think that we have carried one biological body for the duration of our life, but our perception of the world around us is its own evolution and varies considerably over the course of our life. It is like each day we wake up, we are reborn with a new life, with a different consciousness and capability that is stitched onto the day that came before it, then die again once we fall asleep. Because of our own mental evolution over time, it is important to constantly reassess what we believe and hold to be true. Perhaps we do not and cannot fully realize just how much those first few years of life especially influenced the way we connect ourselves to the rest of the universe. Perhaps we are holding onto something traumatic we witnessed when we were two years old and the imprint has been following us for years because we cannot resolve it with what we believe now. To be at peace with ourselves and our surroundings, we must be at peace with not just what happened before we were born, but all that unfolded in our earliest years, recognizing that we had a different kind of alertness and awareness during that time we were not able to yet question or reason around.

However, whatever did happen to you in your earliest years helped you be exactly the person you are today, in all your glory and beauty. It brought you to this moment. Everything that happened, whether you perceive it to be good or bad, has been a silent assistant to you in your life, pointing you toward the new ways in which you are now able to become conscious. Now, as much as ever, is the time to wake up.

What Are You Afraid Of?

Most of our fears, whether it is a fear of heights or fear of another living creature, stem from a fear of death. Even a fear of public speaking might be thought of as a fear of death to the ego and death to control over what other people might think and perceive of you. Whatever you find yourself feeling afraid of, a concept of death is likely just underneath the surface. There are so many ways this can manifest. One thing worthwhile to realize is that the inevitability of change itself, of our perception of time unfolding, of cause and effect, is in and of itself life and death. Every single new moment you experience is life, and the "you" in the moment that has recently passed is already dead to you. The amount of these "mini lives" we have experienced are indeed infinite and are at the nexus of the miraculous infinite gift that we continue to receive right now. If you are one of those who wonder about the ultimate meaning of life, consider it to be death. Your infinite gift has no meaning without the presence of death. As light has no meaning without darkness, life has no meaning without death. One of the final hurdles to being in love with your life is to also love death. If we can love the death of small things, letting go of an argument we had with someone yesterday, letting go of the person we once were a year ago, and even letting go of clinging to the positive experiences that are no longer in existence, then we can eventually come to a place where we can love the fact that our bodies will one day die. Just as the cells in our bodies are dying regularly to ensure the other trillions of cells are kept healthy and ready, our human form will one day die as well so that the greater human organism and all of life might keep itself healthy and ready, realizing ever different and layered levels of consciousness.

Make no mistake about it: you were intentionally brought into being and manifested exactly the way you are so that you could serve as a cell, both infinite and small, in the larger framework in this universe's existence. Being born as a human has provided you additional challenges and hurdles for your human mind that are not seen by most other species, but these challenges also allow you the ability to realize this truth. How amazing is that? Your moment of bodily creation, your moment of bodily death, and all moments in between were all manifest from infinite, pure ordered energy along with the balances and layers of possible order it keeps in check. Remember this above all else. To be truly free during your moments of life is to always keep this close to you. Love it all: love your life and all its "good" and "bad" moments, love the lives of others and everything around you, and embrace and love death. It has already been an intimate part of your existence with every moment you change. It must not have to be something you allow to feed your fears. To be alive each conscious moment with the greatest possible quality and joy is to keep attached to your awareness of the present moment and its mystery. Listen closely to the billions of years of wisdom your body and mind are providing you. It will help reveal to you what it needs to keep ready and healthy. Perhaps just as powerful is the wisdom of those you come into contact with -- either in human, animal or plant form -- that help inform you about what conditions help cause the effect of staying ready, present, and most fully alive. Everything you read, everything you eat, everything you do to exercise your body, everyone you talk to, and everything you watch will either end up guiding you toward or away from an authentic feeling of being alive. One of the most unpleasant things imaginable for anyone is a feeling of deadness in the present moment. But if you happen to be feeling that way, make sure you inspect it and look honestly and deeply around what came before this feeling. If there are people, habits, and things in your life you realize are keeping you from feeling fully alive, perhaps a move away from such influences is needed. If your body and mind are leading you somewhere, even seeming to scream at you inside for change and the death of the condition of something around you, best to follow their lead. Trust in how things will reorient around you in creative and beautiful ways. Remember you are always receiving in the moment exactly what you need, whether you are aware or not.

As we become more and more aware, as we completely let go of the illusion of control and fully trust, we begin stepping outside the awareness of our physical bodies and the thoughts of our minds. We become perfectly synchronized not with our delayed sensory perception of the present moment, but with the present moment itself, which also expands. We spend more moments of our life connected with the part of us that moves at the speed of light, the part of us that is ageless and timeless. It is the part of us we might say is pure spirit, and perhaps part of the dark matter and dark energy we believe makes up a great deal of our universe. When we take a step outside our bodies and minds, we assume the role of observer, the director that is lovingly watching all the movie frames playback and unfold in perfect order and clarity. We watch without judgement, we watch with curiosity, and we watch while we better recognize our complete and unique connection to all spacetime around us. We watch with unbounded love, and we watch with incredible joy and amazement. We watch as we continue to merge more completely with the infinite one.

Epilogue

I once heard an astronaut give a talk and explain that before he went up into space he had a lot of personal anxiety, frustrations, and other problems, but when he saw the vastness and extreme blackness of space alongside the Earth below, he experienced a profound and lasting wave of calm. It was at that moment, he said, that he became aware of how small his problems were and how special we were to be on this tiny planet surrounded by such an incredibly cold and dark expanse. It was only after he was able to zoom out from his day-to-day experience and focus that he recognized his fragility and privilege of being on the glowing blue planet beneath him. The issues he had before seemed to disappear like magic. I met him after his talk and there was a gentle placidness in his eyes as he focused on connecting with me and some students I was with, and thanked me for what I did. For someone so accomplished, I felt nothing coming from him except humility, gratitude, and readiness to receive me. He had touched me deeply just with his being.

My belief is that once someone expands their viewpoint, it is difficult for their mind to "unsee" where they have been. My hope is that after reading this book there are certain things you are not able to unsee, namely the uniqueness of all spaces and times, the ultimate origin for everything in existence, the necessary impermanence for all forms of order, the relative nature of all experiences, the reasons to embrace death, and the incredible history needed for you to be alive and able to read this sentence in this moment. Although these topics were approached from a more scientific slant, I am aware of many of the rich traditions and beautiful books that help guide the world's religious followers. I find all religions corroborating much of the essence of this book and the ways to live a satisfying and impactful life. After considering a number of spiritual texts, I find most all come to similar conclusions: the importance of recognizing that humans and all of life are special, mysterious, and sacred; to take measures to get rid of your ego; to always show kindness and understanding to those around you; to seek peace; to surrender to a power that is higher than you and accept your path; to stay ready; to stay focused on that which has brought you into being and not spend your focus on fame, money, praise, or possessions; to always stay grateful; to build order and discipline around your life; to offer up prayers focused on praise and acceptance of God in your life. Spiritual ideas of good tend to describe ways of being thought to precede elevated collective levels of life-giving peaceful order, and ideas of evil are thought to encourage collective death or disorder to peaceful orders. Most all religions speak of the mystery of being able to have at the same time several distinct entities that stem from only one. All of them talk about the importance of the spirit above the physical realm and the conquering of death through the evolution of new life. There seem to be an endless number of roads, but they all lead to the same eventual destination.

What has been particularly intriguing to me is that from so many different angles of approach and disciplines people are coming to similar conclusions about how we should strive to be. Collaboration seems much more sustainable, stable, and productive over time than is cut-throat competition; truth is prized over lies; seeking war seems to be much worse for the human condition than seeking peace; and there is significant talk about always striving to "be ourselves." We find that seeking too many material possessions and becoming a workaholic often ends in a life filled with feelings of stress, loneliness, and regret. If we are not out in natural settings amongst other life often enough or taking moments to appreciate its wonders, it results in a feeling of disconnection from it. If we do not prioritize truly honoring and being with others in the moment or scheduling in periods of mental downtime, we become exhausted and burned out. If we are not cognizant of the foods, drinks, and medications we are putting into our body, along with our amount of motion and exercise, we can quickly compromise our health and the health of the human collective organism. The absolute most unfortunate type of life in my view is one lived from beginning to end with frequent thoughts of negativity, unfairness and frustration, anger at everything and everyone around you, viewing everything as worthless and pointless, and believing you have no importance or impact on what unfolds around you. This type of rumination prevents you from accessing much more interconnective, healthy, and satisfying ways of being we know are possible. Yet, if it is there inside of you, it is your body's way of telling you what you need to look at but might not want to see. A healthy way of being does not mean that you must feel positive-oriented emotions around everything that happens to you, nor will you, but living with a real-time acceptance and awareness of "what is" greatly reduces the amount of negative energy you may be holding onto and frees up its availability for other purposes. It is all about your seat of focus and how much you are willing to zoom in or out, along with how you see yourself as a servant spirit in the greater web of life and this universe.

As we approach a critical time on Earth where the collective of human existence is borrowing order from so many things at a rate not seen before, it seems necessary for us to slow down a bit and bring greater awareness around our actions and decisions. Just like with the past five major mass extinctions, we must be aware that the Earth and life itself will be just fine going forward without one of millions of species cohabitating it. However we describe our collective behavior toward our environment, referring to it as "saving the Earth" is misleading at best. To be clear, we are prioritizing the preservation of conditions on Earth such that humans are permitted to coexist on it for as long as possible. Of all times to be alive, we are curiously in a unique time in human history where it is possible to transmit and share information and ideas with most anyone around the globe at any time. This means that shared global awareness, along with the ways we are all interdependent, have the real opportunity of becoming much more pronounced with time. But we must not restrict this awareness to humans only and remember the wisdom our biological ancestors and natural surroundings have passed along. Our models of what we count as "growth" may have to be changed significantly as we move forward and become more inclusive for all life forms.

At times I feel overwhelmed by it all, catching myself in moments of dread or fear, but bring myself back to center by being mindful of not holding onto any moment too tightly or for too long. This moment is always exactly the way it is intended to be anyway and never anything else. If the infinite pure energy has conspired to build a creature who might eventually be completely eradicated, as it has done many times before, then we should be accepting of that as a possible outcome as well. The acceptance does not mean apathy, but a deep faith that no matter what humans do as a collective, our particular form of consciousness may be no more one day soon in order to make way for new life. If we trust completely, we can even bring excitement with us around this possibility instead of doom and gloom. We should never underestimate the will of the human spirit, but beyond that we should never underestimate the will of that which created the human spirit. It is inevitable that if the laws of nature continue in their current form, everything in this universe will at some point eventually devolve as certain levels of order will not be able to be maintained, even if that is billions or trillions of years from now.

To maximize the chance of our stable existence for many years to come, above all I believe we need to pay attention to what so many life forms before us have done to thrive over the course of billions of years. They are in tune in sustainable ways that we often overlook. They find a way to eventually form reciprocal, balanced symbiotic relationships with each other, other species, and their environments. If we do not prioritize our symbiosis with the life and resources around us, such as practicing regenerative farming and limiting our amount of land utilization, it all but secures us a short and unstable existence. The world "Earth" starts with the letters "ear", and perhaps this is one indication written into our language that it is something worth closely listening to. The greatest way to realize the ways in which we can sustain our harmony with the Earth is to stay attentive to the present, to have our connectedness to all of life and the universe always top of mind, to stay ready, and to stay healthy. We do not know exactly what we will be called to do in the future, but whatever it is, it will all be important and necessary. Keep your heart open with unbounded love, curiosity, and wonder. Let us eternally seek to more deeply witness and listen together, with full presence to whatever is coming next. Are you ready for your next moment? Then let us begin again.

Acknowledgements

The author is grateful to several people in the writing of this book. Thank you to Madison Wisted, John Schuller, Jean Sloan, and Marcus Huggans for detailing their thoughtful reactions and feedback to the first manuscript. Thanks goes to Matt Ernst, Donna Juliano, and Mari Myers for their editorial changes to this work. Much thanks goes to Susan Peterson and Tom Gindorff for their edits and ideas to improve the manuscript. Thank you to Tyler Krus and David Finley who read the initial manuscript with careful scientific eyes and contributed several ways to strengthen it. Thank you to the conditions created from both the COVID-19 pandemic and racial unrest that erupted following the murder of George Floyd. Without both of these, the motivation and opportunity to write this book would not likely have been present. Finally, much thanks and gratitude goes to my wife and two children for their support, encouragement and patience while I wrote this book. Their love, care, and wisdom have sustained me through many of the darker days in my life, and they continue to inspire and fill me with hope, laughter and joy.

Made in the USA
Monee, IL
28 June 2025

19886149R00121